suburbia

suburbia

A FAR FROM ORDINARY PLACE

DAVID RANDALL

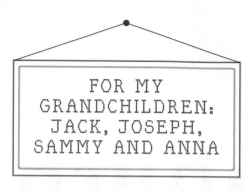

FOR MY
GRANDCHILDREN:
JACK, JOSEPH,
SAMMY AND ANNA

First published 2019

The History Press
97 St George's Place, Cheltenham,
Gloucestershire, GL50 3QB
www.thehistorypress.co.uk

British Library Cataloguing in Publication Data.
A catalogue record for this book is available from the British Library.

ISBN 978 0 7509 9150 6

Typesetting and origination by The History Press
Printed and bound in Great Britain by TJ International Ltd

contents

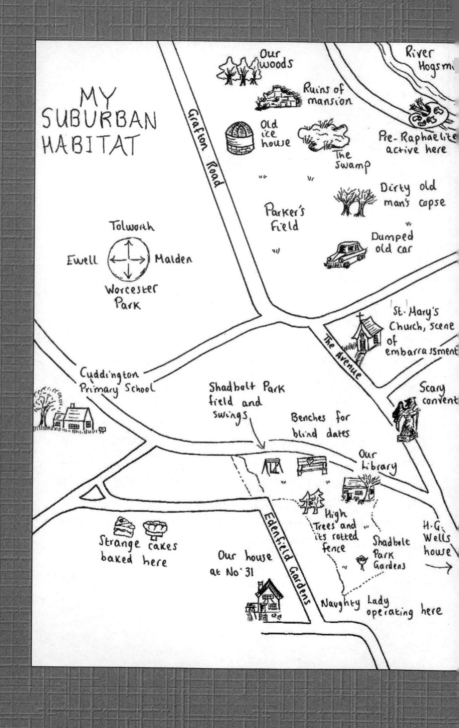

preface

This is a book about the suburbs, and what it was like to grow up in one of them in the 1950s and 1960s. It was written for two reasons. First, to capture that experience of a world now largely lost – its absurdities and happinesses, scandals and follies, and inhabitants both sage and silly. Second, to set down some sort of rejoinder to all the disparagement of the suburbs produced by the writing classes down the years, a strain of rather snobbish metropolitan thinking which is detailed in Chapter One. I've always found the best way to disarm critics is to concede that they may have a point. When the great American journalist H.L. Mencken received letters disputing, often in far from temperate tones, something published under his name, he would send them his standard reply: 'Dear XY, You may be right. Yours sincerely, H.L. Mencken.' The critics of the suburbs may be right, but this book is a small quibble with them, a suggestion that for many of us these areas have been a warming seed-tray in childhood, a reliable base camp for later, tentative, forays into the world, and a place, by and large, of some contentment. My childhood was spent in what now seems a sort of long-lost, semi-detached Shangri-La. Yet all habitats in which you grow up mark you indelibly, and suburbia marked me, not always for the better, I fancy. Here is what happened there.

David Randall
South Croydon, 2019

ONE

the
suburbanophobes

One of the great staples of English fiction over the last century or so has been the character yearning to break free from the oppressively humdrum confines of suburbia. The city, or rather their fantasy of it, seems full of opportunities to throw off the shackles of semi-detached conformity. They imagine that here, amid the bustling anonymity of a metropolis, they will find themselves – liberated at last from the smothering narrowness of Acacia Avenue. And so, exiting towards the bright lights, possibly in some sudden it's-now-or-never haste, goes our hero or heroine.

One of the very first examples of this genre was set in a thinly disguised Worcester Park, the outer London-cum-Surrey suburb where the events of my book take place. It was written by H.G. Wells, who knew the suburb well, having lived there in the 1890s with Amy Robbins (always known to him as Jane), the woman for whom he left his first wife Isabel, and who became the second Mrs Wells. His house was called Heatherlea, a large villa in The Avenue, the long, broad, tree-lined road that wound its way up the hill from the station to St Mary's Church. The suburb in his book is called Morningside Park, the name being more or less the only thing about Worcester Park he changes. The principal characters live in a house very similar to his own, in a road also called The Avenue, and the geography of his fictional suburb is exactly as it would have been then in reality.

The novel is called *Ann Veronica* after its heroine, who is just the kind of young woman – intelligent, beautiful, but vulnerable to the approaches of older, more experienced men as she tries to cast off from her moorings – that got Wells' blood racing. Indeed, in this she bears a resemblance to Amy Robbins, who was his student when they began their affair, and also, in a milder way, to Amber Reeves, his mistress at the time he was writing the book. The latter was twenty-one years his junior and, the same year *Ann Veronica* was published, she bore his child, a daughter.

In the book, Wells writes that Morningside Park was a suburb 'that hadn't quite come off', invariably taken to be a criticism but more likely a reference to the place being still largely undeveloped forty years after the railway arrived. Ann Veronica Stanley, to give her full name, is a 20-year-old student who lives in a large house with her widowed father, a man of business in London, and his spinster sister. She longs to take up her studies at Imperial College, but her father disapproves of the teaching there and forbids it. She wants to attend a fancy-dress ball in town, but her father forbids it, and this is her breaking point. She bolts, borrows money from a heavy-breathing financier who later tries to force himself on her, joins the suffragettes, gets arrested and imprisoned after a demonstration, and then submits to returning home and becoming engaged to an older, overly upright and besotted

Morningside Park neighbour. Her father, still the controlling sort, relents and allows her to attend Imperial College, and there, having broken off her engagement, she falls in love with a married demonstrator, implores him to possess her in terms that shocked several of the book's reviewers, and runs off with him to Switzerland. Although early in the book she utters three lines of exasperation with Morningside Park ('Ye Gods! What a place! Stuffy isn't the word for it!'), what she really wants to break free from is not the suburb, but the restrictions imposed by her father. In terms of what she wants to get away from, the setting is irrelevant: her name might as well be Elizabeth Barratt and her home in Wimpole Street. But then, that seems true of many 'goodbye dull suburbia' novels. What's being fled is not so much a certain kind of bricks and mortar and their ambience as something the main characters, or someone else, has done to bugger up their chance of happiness. It's the suburbs as scapegoat, quite often.

The fictional character most associated with the suburbs is not one who rejects, but instead positively wallows in them: Charles Pooter, of The Laurels, Brickfield Terrace, Holloway, unintentionally funny star turn of *The Diary of a Nobody* by George and Weedon Grossmith. Mr Pooter, a clerk in the City, is socially gauche, pompous, and thinks himself a cut or two above tradesmen, shopkeepers, office juniors, and the rather dubious young women his wayward son Lupin brings home. Lupin and the two men Pooter thinks of as his friends, Cummings and Gowing, regularly take the mickey out of him, and a series of accidents and mishaps play incessant havoc with his dignity. His wife Carrie is the sole person to take him at his own value, sharing his hilarity at bad puns and his preoccupation with domestic trivia. He occasionally gets the better of life, but in general it's a succession of banana skins on which he never fails to slip. Only at the end – in seven chapters added later to bring the work up to book length (it began life as a serial in *Punch*) – do these pratfalls cease, and Pooter emerges with pay rise, promotion and bonus: professional, if not social, triumph.

The book is funny, but knowing something of the Grossmiths' background can stifle the guffaws. This, after all, is fun at the expense of a man of limited education, means and horizons being had by two men of decidedly superior social cloth. The Grossmiths – boarding school educated, both successful theatricals, one also an artist and a member of the Garrick, Beefsteak and Savage clubs – were movers in the sorts of metropolitan circles that have ever since tended to chuckle up their sleeves at the poor little untalented, un-chic people in the suburbs. But at least the Grossmiths seem, in the end, to have found a measure of affection for their hero. They were benevolent satirists. Not so with what followed. The gentle fun that the Grossmiths poked was very soon the least of it. It became a sort of badge of belonging for many writers and intellectuals to forcefully condemn the suburbs and those who lived in them.

Barely more than a dozen years after *The Diary of a Nobody* was published came a book written by Thomas William Hodgson Crosland, a strange individual who combined writing poems full of Christian charity towards the downtrodden with a vicious homophobia that led him to repeatedly try and get Oscar Wilde's literary executor, Robbie Ross, prosecuted for homosexuality. Crosland's book, *The Suburbans*, is so vehement (one imagines his pen digging ever harder into the paper as he wrote it) that it reads almost like a send-up of literary folks' animus against the people who live in semi-detacheds (or 'half-houses' as he called them). Here he is in chapter one, for instance, as he starts to get up a head of antagonistic steam:

> To the superior mind, in fact, 'suburban' is a sort of label which may be properly applied to pretty well everything on the earth that is ill-conditioned, undesirable, and unholy ... The whole of the humdrum, platitudinous things of life, all matters and apparatus which, by reason of their frequency, have become somewhat of a bore to the superior person, are wholly and unmitigatedly suburban.

The poet Hilaire Belloc (great-grandson of Joseph Priestley, president of the Oxford Union, essayist,

MP, and resident of a West Sussex windmill) soon joined in with a versifying shudder at the suburbs:

> Miserable sheds of painted tin,
> Gaunt villas, planted round with stunted trees,
> And, God! The dreadful things that dwell within.

Then there was George Orwell (an old Etonian, admittedly not of the 'Swing, swing, together' boating song sort) putting into the mouth of George Bowling in *Coming Up For Air* these angry words:

> You know how these streets fester all over the inner-outer suburbs. Always the same. Long, long rows of little semi-detached houses ... as much alike as council houses and generally uglier. The stucco front, the creosoted gate, the privet hedge, the green front door. The Laurels, the Myrtles, the Hawthorns, Mon Abri, Mon Repos, Belle Vue ... A line of semi-detached torture-chambers where the poor little five-to-ten-pound-a-weekers quake and shiver, every one of them with the boss twisting his tail and his wife riding him like the nightmare and the kids sucking his blood like leeches.

So it went on. Jonathan Miller (St Paul's School, and Cambridge, actor, doctor, writer, theatre and opera director) invoked the suburbs to express his intense dislike of Margaret Thatcher, and condemn her for her 'odious suburban gentility and sentimental, saccharine patriotism, catering to the worst elements of commuter idiocy'. And Cyril Connolly (Eton and Oxford, writer, editor of influential literary magazine *Horizon*, whose grandfather owned Clontarf Castle, County Dublin) put in his two guineas' worth: 'Slums may well be breeding grounds of crime, but middle class suburbs are incubators of apathy and delirium.'

In his otherwise marvelous book *After the Victorians*, the writer and academic A.N. Wilson (prep school, Rugby, New College, Oxford, son of a colonel who became managing director of the Wedgwood pottery firm) wrote this of the suburban homes built in the 1930s, where live the 'mortgage slaves' as he calls them:

> Each had a scrap of garden behind its privet hedge. Many had a garage. Once inside them, though, and you find that the rooms are poky ... miles from anywhere or anything which could be described as interesting. What hopes these miserable little dwellings represent, what spiritual and emotional constriction they must have offered in reality, as hubby went off to the nearest station each morning ... and the wife, half liberated and half slave, stayed behind wondering how many of the newly invented domestic appliances they could afford to purchase ... No wonder, when war came, that so many of these suburban prisoners felt a sense of release.

Thus, come September 1939, these limited people, doomed never to know the income and lifestyle of the Wilson household, cheerily embraced the liberating possibility of death or maiming rather than face another humdrum day in a semi-detached. Hmmm.

These are not the voices of people having an aesthetic quibble with the use of half-timbered gables on semi-detacheds, faux Jacobean windows on a villa standing in its own shrubberied grounds, or the indiscriminate use of pebble-dash. These are sneers about something way beyond house design. What you suspect to be at work is what we now call virtue signalling: benchmarking themselves as a metropolitan, a sophisticate, a bit of an intellectual player, by showing contempt for those who are none of those things and who've made the basic style error of moving into a home built on the outer edge of some city. It reads like snobbery, but I fancy it may also be unconscious resentment coming out on the page – the always dissatisfied thinking classes irked by what they imagine are the lives of contented, unthinking ones.

I first came across such superior attitudes on, of all things, a youth hostelling holiday in Surrey. My brother Mick and I, then about 16, had gone on a little walking tour, and, being us, began with nothing more adventurous than a short train ride to Westhumble, the station that serves Box Hill. We rambled along a South Downs ridge, and, late afternoon, came to Abinger Hammer, the village and its famed watercress beds hugging one of the less arterial sections of the A25. We wandered into a tea-rooms and sat down. At the next table were a middle-aged couple, and, seeing our hiking gear, they asked us if we were by any chance intending to spend the night at nearby Holmbury St Mary youth hostel. We were, and, as ill luck would have it, so were they.

We had ordered tea and bread and butter and were about to start eating it when up piped one of our fellow walkers. 'I see you're eating white bread,' he said. 'Nasty stuff, white bread. We always have wholemeal.' Did we realise the difference? they asked. I suppose one of us, probably me, must have been foolish enough to say we didn't, and so began a lecture on the benefits of brown bread, and the evils of the baking conglomerates that made the white stuff. We chomped away as they spoke, and might, if they'd gone on much longer, have begun to feel a little guilty. But the woman had seen me put two spoonfuls of sugar into my second cup of tea. 'Ugh! Cancerous white sugar! Didn't you know?' I didn't, and wouldn't have been bothered anyway, 16-year-olds generally not having reached the age when they worry about developing terminal illnesses. They were, they told us (although by now it must be obvious), *Guardian* readers. Which paper did I read? '*The Times*, at school,' I said. 'But we have the *Daily Express* at home.' I might as well have said that our family regularly practised cannibalism. There followed an imploring to try *The Guardian*, and, for some reason, an extended paean of praise for its music and theatre critic, Phillip Hope-Wallace. (Years later, when I'd got to Fleet Street, I saw Hope-Wallace holding court in El Vino, pausing occasionally to eat a sandwich. I'd love to report it was made of white bread, but not being a wholemeal obsessive, I didn't notice.)

This appalling couple were still banging on about *The Guardian* as we trod our way up the lane to the youth hostel. The following morning at breakfast we managed to sit as far away from them as possible (they would no doubt have been disgusted at the cornflakes Mick and I wolfed down). But, as we made to leave, they ran us down, made small talk, and then asked what they'd clearly been itching to enquire. 'So where exactly do you come from?' We told them. 'Ah,' the man said, 'the suburbs.' And they exchanged glances. 'We're in town,' he said, making it sound like Belgravia Square. 'North of the river. Barnsbury.' We didn't give them a chance to elaborate further on their smug gulch. We shook their hands, bade them a lukewarm farewell, and made for the nearest bus stop and home. They damn nearly put me off *The Guardian* for life.

In my twenties, I would occasionally come across condescension similar to that of the Barnsbury Two, but it was only when I went to work in national newspapers, at the end of that decade, that I found this geographical one-upmanship in full vigour. This was especially the case among columnists and the fancier feature writers, the sort who mistook the invitations they received as part of their job as evidence that they had the makings of a boulevardier. There are, I discovered, few groups so slavishly attached to an aura of fashionability than these. No estate agent has a more acute ear for the social nuances of where one lives. For them, to live outside the reach of the London Underground was to be beyond the pale. Several editors and senior writers I knew used the word 'suburban' as a term of all-round condemnation, and, if it came out in conversation where I lived (the outer suburb of Croydon), it was all they could do to keep a straight face. To them, 'suburb' and 'suburban' were words synonymous with the dreary, conforming, dull and small-minded. To live in a suburb was, to their oversensitive postcode antennae, to be ordinary, unadventurous, cosy, limited, unimaginative and achingly unfashionable. As someone who has lived in the suburbs all but two years of his long life, all I can say in response is that they may be right; although quite why these things should annoy them so much is a bit of a mystery.

Suburb-sneering by the self-consciously smart is unlikely ever to disappear. But some of the atmosphere of antagonism is starting to change, mainly because of what is happening inside the suburbs. They were always more architecturally varied than the critics made out (half an hour's walk around one would have told them that), and now they are far less socially uniform than they were. In our part of 1950s and 1960s Worcester Park, there were few terraced homes and flats; almost every man had a white-collar job; there was not a black face to be seen; and it was overwhelmingly Anglican, by sentiment or background, if not attendance. Contrast this with where I live now, in South Croydon, which, within a mile or so of my home, has 1920s and Victorian terraces; semi-detached and detached villas ranging in age from Edwardian to 1950s; a parish church, plus ones for Baptists, Methodists and most other variants; an Oddfellows hall; Pentecostal tabernacle; mosque; retirement homes; and several blocks of housing association flats – a complete jumble of habitats, few of which remotely match the clichéd suburbia. And, in the ten homes nearest my own 1920s terraced house, I have four neighbours of ethnic backgrounds different to my own. This is now not unusual. In Harrow and Pinner, for instance, both part of John Betjeman's Metroland, some 69 per cent and 38 per cent of the residents respectively are of ethnic minority origin. This is another reason why the criticism is becoming muted: it's one thing to sneer at the Pooters, or take a swipe at the Tomkinson-Smyths up their long, gravelled drive, but quite another to lay into the inhabitants of the diverse, multi-faith, multi-ethnic places the suburbs are becoming. Few of the older suburbans would credit political rectitude with bringing them a benefit, but, in this sense, it has.

TWO

a small scandal
in suburbia

In 1953, we (Mum, Dad, and my twin brother Mick and I, aged 2) moved from Ipswich to Worcester Park, a suburb where outer London meets Surrey. Mum and Dad were entitled to think that here, among homes with decent-sized front gardens and plenty of crazy paving, moral standards were high and crime non-existent. This swiftly proved not to be the case. A few days after we moved in, with my father having long since made his bowler-hatted way to the station and thence the office, there came a knock at the door. Mum opened it to find an overcoated man, who raised his trilby, bid her good morning, and announced that he represented the *Sunday Pictorial* newspaper. Had she, he asked, noticed any comings and goings at a detached house diagonally opposite? She hadn't. Had she seen cars delivering young women to the house? She hadn't. And when he tried another tack, she explained that we'd only been here a few days. Off he went, empty-notebooked, and, judging by the number of front gates that bore a little brass plate reading 'No hawkers or circulars', he would have learned little from the good housewives of Edenfield Gardens.

Not much more than an hour passed before there came another knock at the door, and she went through the same rigmarole with Reporter Two. She was by now somewhat perturbed. What manner of road was it they had moved into that attracted the attentions of the more lurid Sunday papers? Mum and Dad took the *Sunday Express*, features on wartime derring-do more its speciality, but she was well aware that there were other Sunday newspapers which took a keen – almost scholarly – interest in wayward Scout leaders, choirmasters with unusual ways of showing an interest in boy sopranos, and other outwardly respectable folk who had faced temptation and succumbed. Mum knew none of the neighbours, and tapping on their door to ask for full details of what had attracted the pressmen was not quite the way she wanted to introduce herself. (People kept themselves in check and at a distance hereabouts. It was, for instance, more than a dozen years before Mum and the lady next door agreed that they would no longer call each other Mrs Randall and Mrs Eyles, but Doris and Beryl. Worcester Park was that kind of place. Less a culture of keeping up with the Joneses, than keeping them at arm's length.) So it wasn't until the local paper carried the court case involving the woman who lived diagonally opposite that all was revealed. She had, in a detached house largely hidden from view by a cordon of conifers, been carrying on a lucrative line in abortions – then illegal. With Britain's most famous amateur abortionist (and murderer), John Reginald Christie, only recently hanged at Pentonville Prison, it was quite a jolt to realise that the same trade, albeit with non-homicidal outcomes (at least for the mother-to-be), was being practised in Edenfield Gardens.

Happily for Mum, the abortionist was not typical of local residents. For many years, all was seemliness, and it was not until halfway through the next decade that a shiver of gossip next ran down the road – and this time Mum was in the know. A married resident had been arrested in a Kingston-upon-Thames public convenience for 'insulting behaviour', legalese for seeking or offering a homosexual act (then outlawed), but also the standard charge by which evidence-inventing police fitted up some hapless chap. The reaction in the road was exactly what none of the rougher Sunday newspapers would have anticipated. There was no tut-tutting, pursing of lips, or anything remotely approaching shock. Instead, everyone we knew had a good chuckle. Unkind, but true. After all, what we later learned to call gay were then 'queers' or 'nancy boys', comical figures who, to us, were either prancing effeminates (as seen on stage and screen), or blokes like our hero who, while living with his wife and children, harboured yearnings which eventually inspired him to hang around the gents in Kingston for the chance of a bit of 'man love'. Neither legalising their activities, fearing or resenting them, nor, for that matter, celebrating them, crossed our minds in the early 1960s. Homosexuals were too far outside the conventional for that.

A lot of things were beyond the Worcester Park pale. Divorce, for one, and we knew no one who had anything other than a full set of parents in residence, and no friend ever reported their home echoing to the sound of flying crockery or other serious domestic unpleasantness. Anyone seeking to understand the social atmosphere of the 1950s and '60s could do worse than consult divorce statistics for that and subsequent periods. In 1958, there were, for a population above 50 million, only 22,654 divorces. By 1969, this had risen to 51,000, and then, in 1969, came the Divorce Reform Act, which allowed couples to divorce without proving adultery or cruelty. That, and a big reduction in the stigma attached to a broken marriage, meant that, just three years after the Act, in 1972, divorces totalled 119,000 – quadrupling in just eleven years. By 1993, there were 165,018 divorces, more than seven times the number in the late 1950s.

There must have been passions behind the painted front doors of these streets, but we knew no one who had them, let alone showed them; no one who had what we now call 'issues'; no one who raised Cain, nor even their voice. And we certainly didn't know anyone who had a sex life. This rather goes against the grain of the Great Suburban Cliché, part of which promoted the belief that illicit couplings were discreetly widespread down any street where flowering cherry trees grew. Milkmen and other tradesmen, went the legend, would be lured into homes by wives in quilted housecoats, and emerge half an hour later, red-faced and with another sure-fire address to tell their mates about. Au pairs from Europe would be ever-ready to induct husbands and older sons into their uninhibited Continental ways. And behind curtained picture windows, house keys would be tossed into empty salad bowls, lots drawn, and wives swapped – a feast of sex on Wilton carpets and velour settees as cost accountants and beauty product demonstrators, project managers and dental technicians cast off the oppressive conformity of their suburb and gave in to desires that had been bottled up for too long. The reality, of course, was that part-time orgiasts were very few in number. For the housewife at a loose end, coffee mornings and outings with the Townswomen's Guild were more Worcester Park's style.

Nothing more typified the daily absence of drama than the daily drama on the radio, *Mrs Dale's Diary*, whose defining feature was that very little happened. The humdrum doings of this doctor's wife and her family in the Middlesex hinterland were thus truer to life than today's soap operas, in which sensations abound, and no contentment goes unpunished. Mrs Dale's scriptwriters preferred life unruffled, the only hint of tension being what might lie behind her oft-used opening line about her GP husband – 'I'm rather worried about Jim' – the cause of the concern invariably turning out to be a spot of dyspepsia, or wilt on his begonias, and not, as it would be today, morphine addiction or the discovery he had a transgender lover. About 7 million listeners tuned in every day to follow what, in fact, needed very little following, and it was only later in the 1960s, when the BBC decided to pep things up a bit with fatal accidents and some mild hanky-panky among the Dales' relatives, that the audience began to drift away. By then, Ellis Powell, the actress who played the title role for the first fifteen years, had gone. Sacked on account of her alleged over-fondness for a sherry or three, she worked briefly as a demonstrator at the Ideal Home Exhibition and cleaner at a hotel before dying three months later at the age of 57. The BBC dealt with this, as they did with all unpleasantness, in true suburban style by the simple expedient of never referring to it.

Worcester Park was a district which began, as so many suburbs did, with the pushing onwards and outwards of a railway. The London and South Western Railway (terminus at Waterloo, major junction at Wimbledon) decided to extend their line to reach Epsom, and, in 1859, where the pioneer tracks ran on a bridge over the road between Cheam and Malden, they put a station, even though there was nothing much there save for a couple of farms. Originally called Old Malden (because that was the nearest named place), it was later re-christened Worcester Park, since, in the days of Nonsuch Palace (three miles to the south-west, and pulled down in the seventeenth century), the Earl of Worcester had been steward of the hunting park whose deer and chases had long since been replaced by cattle and farm tracks.

The first houses unconnected with farming were a terrace of workman's cottages built a quarter of a mile south of the station in what was later called Longfellow Road (Prime Minister John Major grew up in a bungalow a little further down this road). Some shops and villas went up alongside the Cheam–Malden road, and a post office, hotel and other necessaries were built around three sides of a curious little square the other side of the main road from the station. On a new roadway due west of the station, and leading up a gentle rise to where St Mary's Church was later built, large detached villas with coach-houses appeared. And that, a little modest extension apart, was Worcester Park until, in the 1920s, electrification of the train line led to farms selling great swathes of land for housing. Over the next fifteen years, homes and a main road of shops went up, and the Worcester Park we knew was created. But as with most suburbs, you needed to be a resident to tell where ours began and ended, for it merged (or, rather, seeped) into North Cheam and Stoneleigh to the south, Ewell to the west, and New Malden to the north and east. Our home was on the western side, in Edenfield Gardens, about a third of the way along this scale geographically, and half the way architecturally, and so socially. People here were remarkably similar in outlook. Our road might well have been the reservation created by the authorities for a particularly small and homogenous tribe.

THREE

and where do your people come from?

Throughout my childhood, the people I knew were drawn almost exclusively from our side of Worcester Park. I knew no one higher on the social scale than the inhabitants of our area's detached homes, and no one from anything all that much meaner than our semi. There was, briefly, when I first went to grammar school, a friendship with a boy who lived the other side of Central Road in – or, to Mum, dangerously near – some council housing. He dropped his aitches (and, correspondingly, pronounced the letter h as 'haitch'), both worrisome traits to my mother who, for a time, threatened me with elocution lessons if I picked up any more bad speech habits. But, this lad apart (and the friendship soon withered and died, as they do when you're 12 or 13), I never knew anyone from a different background or who spoke differently.

About the only time I encountered grown-ups who worked with their hands, as opposed to wearing a suit and sitting in an office, was when plumbers, electricians and the like came to install or repair something. These seemed nice enough, but, from a young age, I was made aware of what Mum regarded as their difference from us. They wore overalls, and had their tea served in the 'workmen's cups' Mum kept for the purpose, thus ensuring that no working-class lips touched the family's utensils. These were even kept on a separate, lower shelf of the kitchen crockery cupboard. Other residents of Edenfield went further. Several would greet workmen with the news that on no account was the house's loo to be used. The men were informed that the local park or a public house no more than a three-minute drive away both had excellent 'facilities', and it would be appreciated if these were used. Thus were their avocado-coloured sanitary ceramics kept unsullied by the proletariat.

My own, very limited, experience of working men was entirely positive. At 16, I was found a holiday job in a garage owned by a friend of my father's. In those days, long before self-service, motorists would drive onto a petrol station's forecourt, and a menial such as myself would emerge from a kiosk, fill up their car's tank from the pumps, and – hoping for a tip – offer to check their oil, or put some air in the tyres. On the first few days, whenever a Jaguar, large Mercedes or something even fancier drove in, I would spring keenly from the kiosk and set about checking oil and tyres, and maybe even offer to give the windscreen a wipe. But I soon learned that the more pricey the car, and the posher the leather-gloved driver of it, the less likely it was that my enthusiastic petrol monkey act would get a tip. These nobs of the road were the ones least likely to say the magic words 'Keep the change', and most likely to quibble over the amount of Green Shield stamps you gave them. If you wanted a decent tip, I soon realised, the person you wanted to drive in and stop by your pumps was a plumber in a battered van, some jack-the-lad taking his new girl for a spin and eager to impress her, or a wheeler-dealer geezer salesman in his company Cortina who'd just had a good day fleecing shopkeepers hereabouts. Thus, apart from the tips, I got an additional reward: a lesson in social expectations.

Other than this, class did not loom large. So when I went up to Cambridge, then even more dominated by the products of public schools than it is now, I anticipated something of a social jolt. It never really came. Some of those who'd been at minor public schools oozed entitlement, but they lacked real self-confidence, the giveaway being their anxious probing to try and find out what school you went to, where your parents lived, and what sort of car they drove. I was taken once to dine at the Pitt Club, the Cambridge equivalent of Oxford's legendary snob tribe, the Bullingdon. Faced, at the end of the meal, with a bottle of port, I handed it on, only for a voice from the other end of the table to boom: 'You've passed it the wrong way, man!' Angered, rather than embarrassed, I could only stare, fuming, at my empty plate, hoping that this prat would come a dreadful cropper at the next point-to-point. It angered me for a long while afterwards, but by the time I'd thought of a suitable reply ('Not during Lent, I think you'll find'), he and I had both graduated.

Loud voices, I then began to realise, were a sure sign of those desperate to assert themselves, be they minor public schoolboys or urban louts. The most extreme case I knew was a journalist colleague whose conversation was conducted in the unmistakably deafening bray of the socially privileged. I once asked him why he spoke so loudly, and he replied, without blush or trace of irony: 'Well, we were brought up in a big house so you had to yell to make yourself heard.' But in general I found that the posher the school, the less likely were its former pupils to be overbearing. At Cambridge, the editor of *Varsity*, the university newspaper, was Jeremy Paxman, whose school was the decidedly upmarket Malvern College. While he may have later been famous on television for the drawling scoff with which he greeted nonsense spouted by the politicians he was interviewing, he was too much the natural journalist to ever play the posh boy, a broad-mindedness he extended to asking me to write a column for his paper. I leapt at the chance. It was my first bit of published journalism.

Old Etonians and Harrovians seemed to have had a particular courtliness instilled. My best friend in college was a charming old Harrovian who, materially, breathed far different air from me. His parents bought him a Bentley for his 21st. They had even more money than my girlfriend's parents, who had homes in two counties. These, too, were pleasant people, but for all the consideration they showed to this oik their daughter Mary Ann had brought home from university, it was always hard to feel anything other than a poor relation when visiting. 'Do you ride?' one of my girlfriend's relatives once asked, a question, I immediately realised, not designed to find out if I had a bicycle. When faced with people like these, and another who looked crestfallen to learn I did not sail either, it was always tempting to ham things up a bit and start talking like a coster and wiping my nose on my sleeve. Thankfully, I didn't – a rare instance of me showing some consideration to Mary Ann, who was not in the least bit snooty.

Periodically, in the years to come, my class hackles would be raised again. An example, when I joined the staff of the *Observer* in 1981: on one of my first days I was introduced to a public-school-educated colleague. 'Oh, hello,' he said. 'And where do your people come from?' I was so stunned by this Bertie Woosterish question that I could only mumble that I lived in Croydon, which was not, I suspect, the locating point in the shires he was looking for. The paper, for all its lefty postures and the progressive stance it took such trouble to present to the world, was stuck in a pre-1960s world of social distinctions. Its male staff were essentially divided, as sportsmen were in Edwardian times, into either Gentlemen or Players. Those who went to public school were Gentlemen; those of us who did not were Players, even if we'd been to Oxbridge. You might, as our grammar-school-educated editor did, change into a Gentleman if you joined a London club or two, in his case the Garrick. I, with a suburban home to rush back to, no spare income available for a West End club subscription, and even less inclination to settle into one of its leather armchairs, remained a Player. It suited me, but it was a bit like being a well-educated governess in a Victorian household: tolerated for your brains but never really clasped to the bosom.

Long before I got to *The Observer*, I got to feel what it was like for the boot to be on the other foot. In my second week as a junior reporter on the *Epsom & Ewell Advertiser,* I was sent to interview a young nurse at the local hospital. She was on the Royal College of Nursing's general council, and was organising a demonstration for more pay the following week. I arrived early, and was reading over some notes in the nurses' home sitting room when there came a small happy commotion at the door. There was my interview: cheeky and pretty, with laughing eyes. I was instantly smitten. I asked questions, she answered, and I soon had more than enough for the purposes of a short, curtain-raising story. This was not, however, what I told her, saying something along the lines of: 'It's a really absorbing story, but I think I need more information to do justice to it.' Pause. Looks thoughtful; then assumes expression that suggests an idea has suddenly occurred. 'I know. Why don't we have dinner tomorrow night and you can tell me more?' Pam fell for it, and I took her out. It was the first time she had ever crossed the threshold of something called a hotel, and, she later confessed, was somewhat bowled over by this, and the triple crown of suburban menu items I ordered for her: prawn cocktail, duck à l'orange and Black Forest gateau. For the first and only time in my life I had come across as a bit of a smoothie.

She was 20, and I was three years older. That, however, was not the only difference between us. My parents lived in a leafy Surrey suburb, hers in a road wedged between the A3 and Raynes Park railway station. My father was a senior manager with a large oil company, captain of the golf club, and reached the rank of acting major with the Cheshire Regiment during the war. Her father was a clerk of the works in the building trade and had been a sapper with the Royal Engineers. Unlike my father, who saw no wartime action from the safety of a patrol installation in Alexandria, Egypt, hers had been in the thick of things in the Middle East and Italy, where he won the Military Medal. I grew to love this plain-speaking, generous man, who was married to a nervous, socially unsure woman who, at the age of 13, had been forced by her stepmother into service as an under-house parlour maid to a charmless and demanding Berkshire Conservative MP. And Pam, especially when thrust into social settings where she was unsure (which was certainly meeting my parents for the first time), was inclined to ham up the Eliza Doolittle aitch-dropping act. I was sufficiently besotted to propose to her after three days; she was naïve enough to say yes, and so it was that the following day we took my parents out for a drink to tell them. Their reaction barely even made it up to chilly, the news being received with a lack of enthusiasm they made no effort to hide. They would have reacted more warmly if I'd told them I'd been fired from the paper for falsifying court reports.

Next morning, Mum came into my bedroom with a cup of tea. She put it down on the bedside table, turned towards the door, and, as she reached it, looked back and said: 'We thought, having gone to Cambridge, you'd have done better for yourself than that.' The door was shut before I could reply. As I readied myself for work, my anger simmered and grew. When it was time to leave, I did so via a tirade against my parents' snobbery, a slamming of the oak front door so hard that it came partly off its hinges, and the overturning of a couple of large flower pots as I stomped off up the front path. I told Pam all, which may or may not have been wise, and we walked round and round a park in Epsom discussing what should be done. Eventually, it was time to do what I'd been dreading all day: return home for the inevitable facing of the parental music. ('What a dreadful tantrum you threw this morning ... How dare you ... never seen such behaviour ... etc. etc. ...') I put the key in the door and stepped into the hallway. Mum and Dad came out of the living room and greeted me as if the last twenty-four hours had not happened. They never did refer to my performance that morning, nor the remark that triggered it. Within a month, they had decided that Pam was indeed pretty special, and remained convinced of it until the days they both died. Class, contrary to what they expected, never came into it, nor has it overmuch in the intervening forty-plus years during which we have produced four sons, and they four grandchildren.

For an unwholesome-looking sort like me, Pam was quite a catch. She had, after all, been voted Miss Motspur Park 1972, and gone on to compete in the Miss England contest. It was at this event that she caught the eye of a photographer who trotted out the old line about setting her on the way to stardom if only she would agree to come to his studio and have a portfolio of pictures taken. Pam, then only 19 and not altogether worldly, agreed. The 'studio' turned out to be an upstairs room in his house, and even then alarm bells failed to ring in her head. Nor did they buzz when the photographer asked her to remove her bikini top – 'an agent will need to see you like this,' explained the helpful picture-taker. But when, after his wife had served tea and biscuits, he requested she shed her bottom half, even Pam twigged that the session was heading into uncharted waters. She declined, said she was not interested in taking her modelling career any further, and fled the scene. A few days later, in the post, addressed to Pam's dad, came old Percy Photographer's revenge – topless Pam immortalised in half a dozen 15 x 12 prints. She was gated for a month.

FOUR

a sheltered existence

The idea that food on semi-detached tables could be something other than stodge and staples began in the 1950s with wider foreign travel and influences like Elizabeth David's book on Mediterranean cooking. But it passed our end of the suburbs by. Our food, and that of any family we knew, was resolutely – culturally – unadventurous. Garlic and spices went untasted and unknown; the only use for rice was to make puddings; salad was composed entirely of iceberg lettuce, cucumber and tomato; spaghetti came in a tin and you had it on toast; bread was white; so was fish; cheese was only Cheddar; and avocado was not a fruit but a colour scheme for bathroom suites. Nothing that was not traditional and British was ever put in front of us: beef (hot on Saturdays, cold on Sundays), cheese on toast, casseroles, steamed syrup sponge and non-alcoholic trifles (sherry being something you drank, and not tipped into food). The limiting factor was not money (Dad earned well), but cultural, the deep-seated lack of adventure that underpinned so much of life in the suburbs.

The suburban timidity was, in the case of our family and several others I knew, allied to a music-hall patriotism that regarded anything foreign as either inherently comic or deeply suspicious. Mum's wariness of anything remotely non-English extended far beyond food. She had no interest in abroad, and no desire to travel there. She spent her entire life in southern England, save for an hour or so's trip across the border into Wales when holidaying in Herefordshire. Dad, who had at least seen Egypt and the coastline between there and England from a troop ship, was equally unenthusiastic about abroad. The upshot was that all our childhood holidays were taken in southern England, and I, infected by Mum and Dad's wariness, did not fly in a plane or visit a foreign country until I was 30. When I did, Mum was on tenterhooks until I – a national newspaper journalist, married with three sons – returned home unharmed and unsullied by the experience.

This lack of adventure has left an indelible mark: on the food I eat, where I like to holiday (the British Isles), the history I read (English, occasionally American, but never foreign), the home I live in (terraced, in Croydon) and my preference for home over away, safe rather than sorry, family rather than friends, and my own bed and bathroom. Other people's houses, at least when you stayed in them, always seemed a sort of honorary abroad, everything strange and you nervous of making some error with the utensils or fixtures and fittings. An early example of this timidity: among some of my contemporaries, one of the more popular hobbies was not fretwork but shoplifting. At my school, there were intermittent reports of this boy and that banned from the corner sweet shop, or even Epsom's W.H. Smith, after they'd been caught trying a little light pilfering. According to my brother, this high rate of detection showed the shortcomings of a grammar-school education: lots of book learning yet inadequate coaching in life's practical skills. His school, a secondary modern, was, in this respect, a far more effective academy, and the result was a reputation for retail thievery that, he had me believe, was second to none.

Inspired by these tales, I decided to try my hand at it. I was at the annual Schoolboys' Exhibition at London's Olympia, and, setting the bar deliberately low, chose as my target one of the small green erasers displayed on a stand of stationery. A stapler would have shown some manly ambition, or even a geometry set in leatherette case, but I thought I'd start small and work my way up. I circled the stand several times and then, when I'd gathered sufficient nerve, sidled up to the box where the erasers were displayed, picked one out, and transferred it to my coat pocket. I walked away as casually as I dared, my heart thumping. I went a yard or so, stopped, turned round, circled the stand a couple of times, then put the eraser back and scuttled away. For by no means the last time, I realised that any possibility of living a little nearer the edge had been thwarted by fear of the consequences if caught, and general all-round suburban timidity.

A prime example of a sheltered existence, at times literally so, was our parents' reaction to weather. Dad was one of life's optimists. If it rained during our annual fortnight's holiday, he was apt – however steady the fall and uniformly leaden the skies – to dismiss it as 'a clearing-up shower'. Drizzle he would jokingly dismiss as 'condensation' caused by the impending arrival of warming sunshine. Mum saw things from a gloomier perspective, the perpetual weather pessimist. 'Sun before seven, rain by eleven' was her motto, and it was part of her meteorological belief system that the reverse was unlikely to apply. Indeed, sunny mornings of imperishable glory were declared 'too bright', and therefore bound to deteriorate. All in all, our parents could well have been the prototypes for those little figures in the barometrically sensitive model houses that used to be sold as souvenirs at the seaside: Dad the summer-clad little man who came out as the pressure rose, Mum the umbrella-carrying, rain-coated little woman who emerged in his place as it fell.

Weather looming so large on her horizon gave rise to several rituals. Forecasts on radio and television were given studious attention and the choicer, lowering bits harvested. News reports came in handy, too. Blizzards, hurricanes, tempests and the like blighting North America were, we were assured, 'heading our way'. (Never having flown, she had an uncertain grasp of the distances involved, but, had I produced an atlas and pointed out that the tornadoes in the Midwest were occurring some 4,500 miles away, I doubt it would have made much difference. The Gulf Stream, of which she was aware from her close attention to weather forecasts, was to her a bringer not of warming air, but a transporter of anything unpleasant.) Some of these incoming elements were merely inconvenient; others more than that. Strong winds were a real worry, their noise troubling her and sometimes making her flinch. Even if all was calm, she could draw on plenty of indications that this happy state of affairs would soon be over. 'The moon's on its back,' she would say, adding ominously, 'sign of wind.' A circle of haze about the moon was another portent that we'd soon be in for a buffeting. It became a low-level family joke in the end, but thunderstorms were not; they were quite another matter. At the first flash of lightning or boom of thunder, Mum would clap her hands over her ears and take shelter in the cupboard under the stairs. To the best of our recollections, neither my brother nor I found this comical or even unduly eccentric. It was just her way. It never occurred to us until we were writing the double-act we delivered at her funeral that this phobia about loud bangs probably had its roots in her spending 1939–45 in London, and thus as a nightly potential victim of the Luftwaffe. During the Blitz, and later, when the V1 and V2 rockets rained down, she would, she told us, seek shelter under the kitchen table, there being in a Streatham flat no stairs and hence no cupboard under them. Perhaps she could be forgiven what seemed to us her excessive caution about thunderstorms when she had faced, at times daily, dangers in the early 1940s that we would thankfully never know.

Even if there was nothing alarming bearing down on us from across the Atlantic, precautions needed to be taken. When we were young, her insistence on us being protected from the elements, which in southern England were never likely to amount to much, was something of a trial. One of the sights of 1950s–1960s Edenfield Gardens, for example, was Mick and me in damp weather walking the streets, hoping no one we knew would see us, wearing misshapen garments made of heavy-duty opaque plastic sheeting. These were Pac-a-macs, first marketed in 1949 with the slogan 'the raincoat in your pocket'. The pictures in the advertisements for them suggested the shiny macs had a certain Gestapo-chic, but our appearance told a drabber story. They did not shimmer, but with their dun colours (yellows and pinks were strictly for girls) and sack-like shape they conferred on the wearer the guarantee of derision from friends. Neither my brother nor I, however golden the day, could leave the house without Mum insisting we take our Pac-a-macs. We looked like kids who'd been bought them by overprotective parents, as indeed we were. Worse, we looked as if we were sufficiently mollycoddled to have to wear them. One of the most memorable parting shots of Mum's, as we left the house on a imperishably sunny summer's day, was: 'Have you got your Pac-a-macs?' We would lie, but she invariably knew, and we would be called back to wedge the things in our pockets (they bulged, never really living up to the claim in their advertisements to 'pack away to the size of a box of cigarettes'). Even more humiliating was when we got away from the house without the wretched things, only to see Mum appear in the park bearing them. 'You forgot your Pac-a-macs,' she would say, her tone of voice implying this was as reckless as omitting to wear shoes. Critics claimed that the macs, with their welded seams and total lack of breathability, were sweaty and unhealthy. To us, this was the least of their drawbacks.

Wellington boots fell into the same category: articles of clothing Mum thought essential protection, but which we loathed. They never seemed to fit very well, and, as you walked in them as you had to, slightly flat-footed, the look was not a good one. This was, of course, many decades before the wax-jacketed, gum-booted faux young farmers get-up had a vogue, especially among urban buyers of four-wheel-drive cars, the kind of people who wouldn't see a ploughed field from one decade to the next. But even if it had not been so, and rural chic had then been all the go, we knew, despite being children, that there would have been no mistaking us for junior members of the county set as we squelched down the road in our black wellingtons.

Mum's cautionary instincts extended to toys. The idea has spread about that the 1950s and early 1960s, lacking computer games and social media, were far more innocent times. The image is of boys of our generation, dressed in short trousers, Aertex shirts and grey sleeveless pullovers, spending our free time doing fretwork, collecting stamps, making things out of matchsticks or sitting cross-legged in a corner contentedly reading a book. This was not entirely the case. Children, especially those with indulgent parents, or ones less risk-averse than ours, could choose from a range of potentially lethal toys. Among those offering you a chance to kill or maim yourself were junior glass-blowing kits, whose boxes promised 'hours of instructive and fascinating fun' as you toyed with red-hot molten glass. In America in the very early 1950s your children could amuse themselves with the Atomic Energy Lab, containing a small quantity of radium, a million times more radioactive than uranium, which was also thoughtfully included. These were, after all, the days when lads wanting to while away a Saturday afternoon by making an incendiary device could nip down to the shops, buy iodine from the chemist and ammonia from a hardware shop, mix them up, and so make themselves an explosive so unstable it could be detonated with the touch of a feather.

The *Boy's Own Paper*, which we read avidly, carried ads for three other hazardous toys: chemistry sets, sheath knives and air guns. A chemistry set might contain all the ingredients to make gunpowder (instructions for this were included), or poisons such as cyanide and copper sulphate, but we had no interest in having one. Some serious learning seemed to be required, besides which, if you couldn't race, fire, ride or whittle with it, we weren't generally interested. A sheath knife, however, would have come in handy, and looked natty hanging from our boyish belts. But there was no chance Mum or Dad would agree to getting us one, and they certainly drew the line at what we wanted most: an air rifle.

We drooled over the ads for them in the *Boy's Own Paper*. 'It's easy to be a real marksman when you own a BSA air rifle,' ran the copy beneath a drawing of a boy brandishing a weapon that looked almost identical to the ones fired by soldiers in the war films we watched. And, failing a BSA, there could always have been a Diana (decent firearms, our friends told us, despite the girly name), or a Webley air pistol – less range, but more concealable. But it was never likely to be, and so we had to settle, if we wanted to handle one of these beauties, for inviting ourselves to the home of our friend Gus, who did have one. If his parents were out, we would stand on the crazy-paved patio of his back garden and take potshots at the metal cover on a chimney sprouting from the roof of a house at the back. A direct hit was good, but especially prized was a glancing blow which made the cover ring like the sound effect in cowboy films when a bullet hit a rock. We were satisfied with that, but inevitably the day came when someone suggested a live target. We would crouch down, remain still, wait for a bird to fly onto his lawn, and then shoot it. I was not keen on this, but a blackbird landed and began pecking about for worms, a boy took aim, and fired. I can see that poor bird now, flapping about on the grass, badly wounded but not fatally so. We watched, unsure of what to do, until someone advanced forward and with the downward stamp of a teenage boot put the thing out of its misery. So, no air rifle for us, and, after the blackbird killing, no appetite for one either.

Thus, little by little, did we come to absorb the timid ethos of Edenfield Gardens. The caution and undemonstrativeness of this had very little, as far as I could tell, to do with that supposedly common cry of the suburbs: 'What will the neighbours say?' – words I never heard Mum or Dad utter. What motivated them was not so much concern about what others might think, but an unwritten code of considerate behaviour. You didn't make noise enough to disturb those who lived around you not because they might think you low or vulgar, but because the street worked best when people were considerate. It sounds Pooterish, and to some may indeed be Pooterish, but there we are. It is a world away from the idea, not modern but often heard now, that some mythical personal 'right' trumps consideration. It's 'my right' to make as much noise as I wish, have a front garden full of rubbish, drop litter, park here, picnic there, or put my feet up on the train seats – an inflated sense of your own entitlement erected into a sequence of mythical rights.

A small example of how the code of consideration worked in practice was the telephone. We had one in our house, but it wasn't entirely ours. The number we had – DERwent 1701 – was ours, and the black handset with its ring of letters and numbers to dial with was ours, but the line into the house wasn't. We shared it with another household, an arrangement called a party line, which meant it could only be used by one party at a time. Thus, wanting to make a call, you picked up the phone and, if there was a dialling tone (a continuous *burrrrr*ing), then away you went with your call. But if you heard voices speaking, then the other party was using it, and back the handset went on its cradle. You might have to pick it up several times over the ensuing ten minutes before you heard they had finished and so freed up the line. Eavesdropping on their calls was possible, but never done by us. For a start, they would have heard a click when you picked up the handset, but none when you failed to put it down. Second, our other party being a church organist called John Avery, his wife and their two young children, the chances of hearing some outrage being cooked up, or the playing out of entertaining argy-bargy, were slim. The other thing telephone users had to contend with before 1958 was the telephone exchange and its operators, to whom you had to speak in the unlikely event of wanting to ring long-distance. You gave them the number and got through after your operator had made what, to you, was a miraculous connection.

It was some time before the party line was replaced by one for our sole use. Further years passed before the direct dialling of any UK number became possible, the old telephone exchanges disappeared, you no longer dialled a combination of letters and numbers, and DERwent (the name for all Worcester Park numbers) 1701 was translated into the more prosaic 337-1701, which in due course became 01-337-1701, 071-337-1701, and 020 8337 1701 – the advancement of telecommunications charted in ever-lengthening numbers. (For anyone wishing to ring me with praise or abuse, please note this has not been my phone number for nearly sixty years.) For the benefit of young readers, we dialled in those days not by hitting a sensitised electronic keypad but by putting a finger in one of the ten holes of a rotary dial and turning it clockwise as far as it would go before your digit hit a small metal arc positioned outside this ring at about four o'clock. Each number 1–9 had three letters of the alphabet beside it (O was for 'Operator'), so that DERwent was, in numerical terms, 3-3-7. The translation of numbers into their alphabet equivalent had its uses. How, for instance, to remember the phone number of a friend of ours notorious for his ability to detect smutty undertones in the most unpromising of material? Easy. His phone number following DERwent was 3825, which, rendered into letters, gave you F, U, K, C, although in a rather more striking order. It was an unfailing aide-memoire.

Our telephone sat in the hall on a small cabinet which had been made for Dad by a German prisoner of war who'd been a furniture maker in Heidelberg before taking up storm-trooping. (Dad superintended an oil terminal and PoW camp in Alexandria, Egypt, during the war.) There was no seat, for lengthy phone calls were not encouraged. Calls were charged by the minute, and the subsequent arrival of an itemised bill showing numbers rung and duration of calls would betray the talkative boy. We soon found that the ensuing brouhaha with Dad was not worth the candle. We learned briskness, especially in bringing a call to an end, a minor art form still not mastered by some even today: a minute or two's worth of repeated 'So there we are's, 'Well, I'd better go's, 'Yeah ...'s and tentative 'Bye, then's before, like the last rites at the end of a lingering death, the final farewell is eventually administered.

But then, in the 1950s and 1960s, the telephone was a strange and unfamiliar device to many. Elderly users were apt to pick up the handset as if it was booby-trapped, and, when they at last spoke, would try an uncertain 'Hel-lo', as if entering a dark and possibly inhabited cave. And some households declined to have a telephone, not always on grounds of cost. My father-in-law refused to have one lest his employers bother him when he was not at work. He would have found the idea of wanting to have a phone in your pocket, permanently with you, profoundly puzzling. His family relied on a call-box down the road, or on the good offices of a connected neighbour whose number was given to relatives on condition that they only used it in the direst of emergencies. This meant that a knock on the door from Mr or Mrs Cousins, their kindly telecoms providers, was thought of as tantamount to a visit from the Grim Reaper himself.

Another part of the suburban code of rubbing along, of living alongside each other in the same road while doing the best not to make your presence felt, was a dearth of what critics think such areas are full of: one-upmanship. Life was not a competition in Worcester Park, in the way it would have been (and still is) among folk higher up the property scale. Or lower, for that matter. In his researches among working-class areas in the Fifties, sociologist W.G. Runciman found this voice, from a male nurse living in Swansea, South Wales:

I'd say we were all working class here, but there's plenty of showing off. If anybody does a bit of decorating or buys something new, they leave the lights on with the curtains open to make sure the neighbours get a good look. And the palaver with the dustbins when they are put out for collection on a Tuesday morning is quite a sight – all the best tins, or bits of expensive vegetables or chicken bones or whatever, stuck prominently on the top where the neighbours can see how well-off the family is, or pretends to be.

(Chicken, astonishing as it may seem, was something of a pricey rarity in the decade or so after the war. It was, even for our middle-income household, enough of a treat to be served with due ceremony for Christmas dinner.)

There was little sign in our area of anyone crowing about anything new in the home. This was not virtue, but because part of the code of our suburb was that such grandstanding would have been thought vulgar, and avoiding that was more important than having passers-by admire your new green velour three-piece suite. It wasn't that we had nothing to show off, more that the showing off would have cheapened it, made it look as if it had been bought merely to score points. In Worcester Park, points were for discretion, for keeping your possessions to yourself, and your head down if at all possible. Besides, buying furniture and equipment for the home was not, as it later became, a sort of continuous process, with, if it was left unaddressed for any length of time, the absence of recent new acquisition becoming a vague itch that grew stronger and stronger until it could only be salved with a splurge at some out-of-town hyperstore.

The exception to this was the new car. Unless you waited until after dark on a moonless night, and had left the garage doors open so you could drive it straight in without stopping, a new car was difficult to hide. Dad made no attempt at concealment, one of his few real indulgences being to buy a new car every two years, invariably a Wolseley 16/60 saloon. On being driven home, it would be parked on the raised driveway, all the better to display its two-tone bodywork and spotless chrome bumpers and radiator grille. Thus, for a day or so at least, our front garden was turned into a one-vehicle motor show, albeit minus cheesecake models draped over the bonnet. Not that Dad would have wanted any young woman, however lithe, lying on his new car. Their clammy flesh and manicured fingers would have 'left marks' and so meant yet another going over with the Simoniz body wax and Autosol liquid chrome polish.

Part of this sheltered existence was that those who lived in places like Worcester Park in the 1950s and 1960s were totally non-diverse. In the way we looked, our nominal religion, our ancestry and our instinctive knowledge of what was expected of us, we were remarkably similar to each other. It was, in a way that no one under the age of 50 can begin to imagine, a very white world we inhabited in the outer suburbs of the 1950s and '60s. We knew no one who was other than Caucasian, people of Afro-Caribbean or Indian subcontinental origin being, in our suburb, simply not seen and certainly never met. There was one boy at my grammar school with skin darker than the rest of us and curly black hair. He was called Nigel, and, after he arrived, it took the playground wags just one glance for the first syllable of his Christian name to be translated into the N-word. It sounds shocking, and is, but these were the days when even *The Guardian* newspaper referred in its reports from America to 'negroes'. If the *bien pensants* of liberal journalism used that word, small wonder that schoolboys used its unpleasant derivative. (Recalling these usages from the 1950s and 1960s underlines the fact that, whatever still remains to be done on the race equality front, at least some progress has been made since those days.)

Our grandmother was the first in our family to experience the beginnings of a multi-ethnic Britain, and she, raised in the nineteenth century and mentally always Victorian, was completely unprepared for it. She had lived nearly all her life when the British Empire was in its pomp – bringing civilisation, as she would have seen it, to primitive natives in far-off lands – but then she started to see from her window that a few of these subject peoples had made their way to south London and begun to settle there. She was bewildered by this, and not a little put out. I remember, during her last illness, we visited her in Bolingbroke Hospital, Wandsworth. While we sat at her bedside trying to think of something to say, a nurse came up and had the following brief conversation with her. Young white nurse: 'Have you had your tea yet, Mrs Randall?' Grandma: 'Yes.' Young white nurse: 'Who brought it for you?' Grandma, answering with all the contempt her old voice box could muster: 'Some black.' And so, having come into this world when the inhabitants of Jamaica were exotic people in picture books, she lived to find them working in her hospital and easing her into the next.

Mum and Dad were slightly taken aback by Grandma's strength of feeling on the subject. But then, living in Worcester Park, never going abroad for holidays, Dad working in a central London office, and with their social lives bounded by the golf club and Townswomen's Guild, they – Grandma's final hospital stay excepted – never encountered anyone who was not of the same race and colour as themselves. So racial diversity, let alone integration, was not even theoretical. They never gave it a moment's thought because it was inconceivable. People of Afro-Caribbean, Indian subcontinental, Far

Eastern, Middle Eastern – or any other kind of, to them, exotic – origin were never met, nor likely to be. They were not individuals, but stereotypes on the books of a sort of global Central Casting, the world south of Dover reduced, for Mum and Dad's generation, to odd and, unless they were fomenting uprisings, essentially comic clichés. And so, in books, comics, cartoons and newspapers, they were pigeonholed and lampooned. Music hall and variety shows were rarely complete without blacked-up singers called N***** Minstrels waving their hands about and periodically crying out in high-pitched voices 'Oh Lordy!' Films of the 1930s had subservient black characters, whose dialogue often seemed to consist of little more than 'Okay, Sah!' as they trotted off to do Whitey's bidding. (An example was an actor and singer whose stage name of Stepin Fetchit made no bones about what was expected of black people at that time. His real name was Lincoln Theodore Monroe Andrew Perry, son of West Indian immigrants to Florida, who grew up to be a comedian billed as 'The Laziest Man in the World'. He did rather well out of this clunky racism, being the first black actor to get a screen credit, and the first to become a millionaire. Unfortunately, he was later also the first to be declared bankrupt.)

The casually insensitive attitudes found in 1950s Worcester Park seeped into the small change of everyday conversation, heard by us at its most

[handwritten margin note: We can say or write Fuck but we can't use nigger in a historical sense? Grow up!]

glaring in Dad's occasional remarks about Jewish people. We didn't consider it antisemitism (although someone Jewish probably would), more a sort of hypersensitivity. You might almost say he had a thing about Jews, which was odd, really, because both the best man at his wedding and his closest chum in later life were Jewish. But this was no bar to him observing of someone who worked in certain industries (jewellery, banking or the rag trade), whose nose was prominent, or who was reluctant to stand their round: "Course, Jewish, you know.' And Dad, once someone had been so pigeonholed, would occasionally spread his arms, hands uppermost, and say, in the voice of a music-hall Hymie: 'My life!' It never failed to amuse him. Even as a child I thought this odd, mainly because I could see no difference between those identified as Jewish by Dad and those who were not. As I grew up, it seemed even odder. Our parents' generation was, after all, the one which had sacrificed several years of their prime – and seen people they knew killed – to defeat Nazism and the most rancid of antisemitism.

Indeed, the war had added first-hand experience to the music-hall caricatures Dad carried around with him as part of his mental luggage. It was gained by the several years he spent in Egypt, and this had not endeared Arabs to him. These, he would explain, were not to be trusted, and he would tell you how army lorries or jeeps driven into Alexandria and parked for a short while were liable to be found, on the driver's return, wheel-less and jacked up on bricks. That the Arabs were an invaded and occupied people whose poverty might have some bearing on their behaviour was not considered.

FIVE

suburban streets

Part of the soundtrack of the suburbs, from early morning to midday, was the whine of the milkman's electric float as it came up the road. It would stop at most houses; there would be the rattle of glass bottles in the metal crate, a *clink* as a pint or two would be put on the doorstep, another rattle, and the whine would resume as 'Milkie' moved on another 20 yards or so. Ours was called Len, and he told us he took this out-of-doors job because of the deprivations he suffered as a Japanese prisoner of war. This was not said in a self-pitying way, trying to suggest that, were it not for his years of imprisonment, he might otherwise be carving a creative swathe indoors through the world of nuclear fission or high finance, but stated as if the one was a self-evidently true function of the other. The precise cause and effect at work here was a bit of a puzzle, but we saw no reason to doubt him. He was a decent, cheery sort. Like all milkmen back then, he dealt in cash, wearing a leather satchel around his waist over his blue-and-white striped apron. By the end of a shift it must have been bulging with money, and it's a tribute to the lawfulness of the times that there was not a trail of mugged milkmen all over Britain.

Part of the folklore about the suburbs, and a device used ad nauseam by low-budget comedy films, was the palpitating housewife, clad only in dressing gown, luring the milkman in to enjoy

or nightie

her favours. 'Oh,' the scriptwriter would have her say, as she simultaneously examines an empty purse and bends forward to show a little more cleavage, 'I haven't got any money today.' Pause. 'But there must be some way I could pay you.' And in would go Milkie, carrying his crate, and – a dissolve and several suitable sound effects later – would emerge adjusting his clothes, only to be observed, of course, by the net-curtain-twitcher over the road. I never heard of such a tableau taking place in real life, nor a milkman ever being cited as co-respondent in a divorce. But the idea that milkmen are bringing something more personal than dairy products to the stay-at-home women of Britain persists, despite there being precious few roundsmen and housewives left to participate in the transaction. It is, I suppose, a question of theoretical opportunity, something denied to other regular house-to-house callers such as coalmen (too covered in black dust), and, for some reason (despite them entering the house to carry out their task), meter-readers, electricians and plumbers. Brush salesmen, too, never acquired an association with daytime hanky-panky. Ours, a representative of the Kleeneze company, appeared periodically at our door, wearing trilby hat, business suit and carrying his suitcase of wares. He had a vaguely ingratiating manner and a simpering smile. He could have been Uriah Heap's nicer younger brother.

As Mr Kleeneze lugged his brushes down Edenfield Gardens in the late 1950s, the road would have had a very different atmosphere to the one it has today. The properties, some updating and the odd extension apart, would be the same, but there would be a number of key changes, not all of them immediately obvious. The two scenes – Edenfield today, Edenfield 1957 – would, if set beside each other, be like one of those 'Spot The Difference' puzzles. Here are ten things you might spot in the earlier of the two pictures:

No hanging baskets. Popularised from the 1980s onwards by gardening magazines, television programmes, overzealous committees in Best Kept Village competitions, and promoted relentlessly by garden centres, they were unknown round our way in the Fifties, and, even if available, would have been regarded as a piece of excessive showiness. And that, in clothes, car, garden, colour of house's paintwork or boastful talk was, in a phrase of the times, 'infra dig', which, rendered into its original Latin of *infra dignitatem*, means 'beneath one's dignity'. And dignity was quite important to the residents of Edenfield in the Fifties. But not excessively so, for that would have been ostentatious, and so, itself, infra dig.

Women wheeling shopping baskets. Wives in 1950s Worcester Park did not, as a rule, have jobs. They were housewives, and, lacking freezers and possibly a fridge as well, went to the shops almost every day. Mum certainly did, and being one of the many wives who did not drive either, this meant a walk and some means of bringing the weighty goodies home. Hence the basket – not the large wire jobs from supermarkets, but a deep canvas bag or wicker barrel on two wheels, with a long handle attached. The idea that there would be a big weekly shop, with husband and wife going to the shops so that provisions could be brought home in the car, was pretty much unknown. I can't recall Dad ever being party to a food shop until he had retired, and not all that often then. This former oil company executive would, after a lifetime of avoiding Sainsbury's, Victor Value and the like, have been as out of his depth as Mum would have been if handed the specifications for a new industrial lubricant.

Far fewer cars. For every ten cars on the road in the mid 1950s, there are more than 100 today. And, in areas like Worcester Park, many households with one car in 1957 would now have two, or, if a grown son or daughter is still living at home, three. And, although not all that apparent in the Spot The Difference picture, the cars of the 1950s and 1960s were considerably smaller. The Mini, for example, was then 6ft long; today it is 2½ feet longer. Then it was 4ft 7in wide; today it is 6ft 3in.

Front gardens kept as gardens. In 1950s Worcester Park, every semi and detached house had a driveway and garage. Cars were parked on the driveway when being cleaned, tinkered with, packed or unpacked, but otherwise kept in the garage. Today, after cars have multiplied tenfold but the number of garages stayed the same, front gardens have been commandeered, tarmacked, paved or bricked over to create forecourts on which to park, and display, the household's cars. One suspects there is, in the minds of the owners of today's larger detached homes, the idea that displaying these vehicles might lead passers-by to think that here is a household ripe for the pages of *Country Life*, with the estate's fleet having been brought round to the front. It is the sports utility vehicle as shooting brake, the suggestion that a chauffeur in jodhpurs might soon be called into action.

Hats. There was a formality about dress in the 1950s that would be striking in comparing the two pictures. Men wore suits far more than now, few above the age of 30 sported leisurewear, and no one but the under-25s and workmen ever wore jeans. I never saw my father-in-law, a clerk of the works in the building trade, in anything other than suit trousers, collared shirt, tie and, possibly, a short-sleeved pullover. A summer's day at the weekend might see him shed the tie, but, if he left the house, on it would go again, and his arms put into a formal jacket. Nothing showed this formality more than hats. The mornings would see bowler-hatted commuters making their way to the station, and, at weekends, this dark upturned pudding bowl would be swapped for a trilby, or maybe, for sportier types, a checked or tweed flat cap. Women wore hats if they passed beyond the front door: round, woollen, felt or fluffy things when shopping (unless the day was very warm); and something stiffer and decorated for 'occasions'. And children, even those at state schools, wore caps. Being seen without your cap was a punishable offence at my grammar school, and it was only when I was but a street or so from home, fully 3 miles from the school and confident that masters and prefects were safely elsewhere, that I ever dared remove the thing. I once, in a moment of madness, leant out of the train window with my cap on and watched horrified as it blew off and went cartwheeling down the embankment somewhere between Ewell West and Stoneleigh. I can still recall the terror I felt, not because I would have to tell Mum she'd have to buy me a new one, but because I would have to go capless to school for a day or so and run the constant risk of a detention.

Standard roses. These odd-looking things – all trunk and stake, with a pom-pom of blooms at the top – stood either side of many a front garden path then, but are largely no more. They and the dwarf hybrid tea rose bushes that shed their gaudy petals with such casual ease have gone the same way, victims of the rise of the garden centre and the massively greater choice now available to anyone wanting to colour up the approaches to their front door. In the

Fifties, buying plants meant a visit to a poorly stocked local nurseryman, or, for the serious grower or the garden-proud, going through a process which began with seed catalogues and progressed on to greenhouse, cold frames, pricking out, potting up, nurturing, and far more fuss than Mum and Dad were prepared to go in for. And so our garden, like so many, saw the appearance decade after decade of the same thin assortment of bulbs and perennials: daffs, wallflowers, marigolds, arabis, pinks and roses. It was as if a particularly vigilant preservation society had taken charge of the garden.

Delivery men. Quite a lot of things we now have to go to the shops for were, in the 1950s, brought to the door, or at least to your road. Following the milkman down Edenfield would be the baker's van, a loaf left on the doorstep, and a weekly knock so you could settle up. There was a mobile greengrocer selling fruit and veg from the back of a large army surplus lorry, and every week would come the Corona soft drinks man in a large flat-bed truck laden with lemonade, dandelion and burdock, and one variety which sounded like nectar but proved too sickly even for my taste: cream soda. Mum had no truck with this truck, a glass of diluted squash or water being, she assured us, far more refreshing. (And cheaper, we thought to ourselves.) On Thursday the laundry man would come, bringing a box of newly starched detachable collars for Dad. And for a time, every

Thursday evening, we had a pools man come, the local agent for Littlewoods or Vernons who collected completed coupons and money so that, at 5 p.m. on a winter's Saturday, your forecasts of draws and away wins could be checked as the classified football results were read out on radio's *Sports Report*. Dad, never convinced that any flutter beyond sixpence on a game of golf was worthwhile, soon dropped the habit. And there was also said to be an Avon lady roaming our roads with cosmetics, but we never saw her. She was but a rumour. She might as well have been the Lady of Shallot.

No skips. There was little need in places like Worcester Park for the fronts of houses to be the temporary resting place for these vast iron waste bins. People, at least in the outer suburbs, did not then knock through, have their houses extended, conservatories built, or get the builders in to do wholesale structural alterations. They bought a house, lived in it, maybe smartened it up a bit, and, if they needed a larger one and could afford it, moved. If they wanted a breakfast room, they'd go to a café. If they wanted an en suite bathroom, they'd go to a hotel. And if they wanted a sun lounge, they booked into a seafront one. It had not yet occurred to them that the house they'd bought was merely a jumping-off point, something you could expand and alter so much that even its own builder would not know it. And so, in the outer suburbs, skips were unknown. Besides, the idea of having your old bath lying for all to see outside your house would have been regarded as vaguely indecent, like letting the neighbours catch sight of you in your dressing gown.

Rag and bone man. Here he would come to his horse and cart, alerting housewives of his approach by singing out the name of his trade, a sound which, in the way of street cries, came out – with a slight musical lilt – as something like 'Raguhbowne!' It only occurred to me years later that, while suburban women might have some old, unwanted clothes, very few, if any, would have had much of an accumulation of bones to dispose of – serial killing, then as now, rarely being a pastime followed at home. What our rag and bone man collected, judging by what piled up behind him on his cart, were metal objects and old tools, the rags and bones of his trade's name being a carryover from the past when old clothing was often sold to artisan paper makers, and bones to soap makers. By the late 1960s, the totter who scavenged Worcester Park had similarly passed into history.

Dogs' mess. The idea of dog walkers following their animals about with a plastic bag in which to scoop up their faeces was completely unknown. And so, one of the last items you would have spied in the 1957 Spot The Difference picture would have been the turds lying on the pavement, waiting for the unwary to step on them. And all of us quite regularly did. The lack of dog shit now, despite the increase in the number of dogs, is, for those of us old enough to remember the bad old turd-filled days, a small sign of progress. Not quite up there with preventative dentistry, but welcome all the same.

Worcester Park was not (few suburbs are) an estate of identikit homes. Different builders working in slightly different years, with the need to appeal to the full range of commuters (from clerks up to stockbrokers and other men of substance and means), meant there was no set pattern to the homes. Parallel to the railway line, and heading up the hill whose summit divided Worcester Park from Stoneleigh (another railway creation, only later) were a few streets of near-uniform small semi-detacheds. But elsewhere, every road contained a jumble of styles: ones vaguely resembling chalets; the occasional bungalow; larger semis; and detached homes ranging up to double-fronted ones with semi-circular drives. All tastes were catered for, from faux-farmhouses with large half-timbered gables, and red-brick ones that looked like small versions of the local telephone exchange, to racier items such as the odd stuccoed interloper with Continental-style (but non-functioning) shutters and lurid green roof tiles – a style you might call Surrey Spanish.

Everywhere you looked there were echoes of the Arts and Crafts movement: half-timbered, black-and-white gables; diamond-shaped leaded lights; and fussy detailing on or near front doors, with odd outbreaks of stained glass in porch windows. Our house had all of those things, plus a curious little oriel window to the bathroom. It also had, at the exposed side and back, another, less happy, fad of the Arts and Crafters: pebble-dash. This was a coating which made a house look as if its builders had spent nearly all their money on the timbered gables and leaded lights of the front and so had to economise round the back and side. Thus our house was, from the front, a pastiche of sixteenth-century Stratford-on-Avon; yet from the side and rear it looked like a dried-up river bed, being coated with ochre-coloured cement embedded with tens of thousands of bits of assorted gravel.

Most homes, like ours, had a number; but some had names. I never saw a 'Dunroamin" or a 'Mon Repos' (just as one never heard of anyone calling their dog Fido or their cat Tiddles), but we did actually have a 'Shangri-La' in our road (a sign to this effect hung over the doorway of a semi made particularly gloomy by brown paint and a front garden beset with conifers). And there was a 'Pantiles', the 'l' of whose sign we longed to have the courage to surreptitiously remove. There were many homes whose owners (or previous ones) had named them after some famous arcadia. Thus, houses stuck resolutely in the soil of north-east Surrey bore at their gates or above their porch such names as 'Windermere', 'Mevagissey',

'Arran', 'Braemar' or 'Anglesey'. Since it was unlikely that a sizable minority of Worcester Park inhabitants hailed from Britain's more attractive Celtic fringes, memorialising a favoured holiday spot was probably the cause.

The motive was another matter. Some who converted their homes from a number to a name probably did so in the hope of adding a smidgeon of value. With others, you suspected, pretension was at work, the house christened with a name ('The Woodlands', Greenfields', etc.) that suggested it commanded several choice Home Counties acres, when all it oversaw was 60ft of untended shrubs. The rather plain detached house next to our park had at some stage been christened 'High Trees', presumably in the hope that utility companies and distant correspondents unfamiliar with the home or its modest road would assume, before they actually visited, that the residence was approached through an avenue of poplars, when it was actually accessed through a wrought-iron gate and 30ft of front garden. Name your house thus, and a supply of Basildon Bond writing paper with the address printed in the top right corner could then be ordered from the local stationers, and no excuse squandered to fire off a letter bearing the impressive address.

The chatelaine of 'High Trees', a Mrs Boddington, was regarded by some as the road's grande dame. The best bursting of her balloon came from my brother who, when she boasted to him that she and her husband were about to take a holiday in the Canary Islands – then regarded as almost impossibly exotic – replied: 'Oh yes. Our milkman goes there.' She was horrified. Her husband, who had a Clark Gable moustache, although regrettably none of the film star's manners, once said in our hearing that semi-detached houses like ours in the road brought down the value of his own detached property. Dad's response, when we told him, was to ask us to convey his thanks to Mr Boddington for the uplift in value to our modest premises caused by sharing a road with his distinguished detached house. Dad didn't really think we'd have the brass neck to deliver this sarcastic message, and he was right. Still, revenge of a more lasting sort was extracted. Mrs Boddington's house adjoined the park and we made it a ritual after an evening at the youth club or the pub to line up as many friends as we could muster and urinate against her fence, giggling all the while. In time, the marks of algae and wood rot were plain to any passer-by. Our mother, who made it her business to know nearly all of our filthy little ways, claimed she could smell it as she made her way past this pissing point to the library.

Street names in Worcester Park lacked the ambition of house names, but made little more sense. Local historical connections were ignored, and, instead, the wilds of Caledonia and the Lake District were invoked: Ardrossan Drive, Kinross

Avenue and names like Glen View were adopted, when the nearest glen was probably 400 miles away. Then there were those names which were a hitching of one pleasant rustic association to another in meaningless combination: Heatherlea, Brookfield, Meadowview, etc. – the permutations for lazy local authority bureaucrats were almost endless. Ours was one of these: Edenfield, to which the designation Gardens was added. In the roll call of words for a road, 'Gardens' comes somewhere in the middle. An order of suburban salubriousness would, starting with the least fancy, go something like: Road, Close, Crescent, Gardens, Drive, Street, Avenue, Lane, Walk, finally climaxing with anything that had a definite article – 'The Avenue' being distinctly posher than a mere avenue with a name attached.

Quite a few houses had front gates, and some of these had signs on them, small metal plates on which was etched a message to callers, actual or potential. Among the most absurd was: 'No hawkers or circulars.' Hawkers was the word used in Victorian times for men peddling goods in the street from a tray, unlikely types to be found going from house to house among Worcester Park's semis in the 1950s. What was meant, of course, was no door-to-door salesmen. The other common sign read: 'Beware of the dog.' This warning was by no means confined to the gates of dog owners, but, with Rover either having gone to the great kennels in the sky, or he and his best friend having moved house, it was left in place as a general deterrent to anyone toying with the idea of approaching the house and knocking on the door. Here, among the semis of Worcester Park, what both the hawker notices and the dog plates actually signified was not so much the literal message on them, but that here lived people who wished to be left alone. All part, I guess, of the suburban reluctance to greet with enthusiasm anything out of routine or unexpected. Then there were others who regarded any foot set on their front path or garden as an unwarranted invasion of their personal space. I have seen the sign 'Private Property' affixed to a suburban side gate, and, while I've never actually heard a semi-detached householder shout at a boy retrieving a wayward football 'Get off my land!', this was the general drift.

This mania for privacy – and many people in the suburbs had it in a far milder form – seems small-minded, and undoubtedly to some extent it was. But something else was at work besides a fetish for pulling up the drawbridge and keeping the rest of the world at bay. In the fifty-seven years between 1914 and 1971, homeowning rose from 10 per cent of all households to 50 per cent. Many of the good folk of Worcester Park and suburbs like it would have been first-generation homeowners, their parents and grandparents having known nothing other than renting.

Small wonder then, after all those years of living in homes owned by someone else, and possibly with communal facilities, that with ownership came an enhanced, probably exaggerated, sense of proprietorship and privacy.

There were times you were in the street when you actually couldn't see the street. Smog – natural autumnal and winter condensation mixing with the particulates and airborne residue from millions of chimneys – was brewed up in central London and spread an impenetrable fog well into the suburbs. Here it joined the native output. Almost everyone heated and powered their homes by burning solid fuel, and as the fog came down the fires were stoked up, and the smog grew thicker and thicker. Visibility was routinely reduced to a few dozen metres, and, in extreme cases (which came at some stage every winter), no more than a few feet. One year, as Dad drove us to spend Christmas Day with my Auntie Doris's family in Beckenham, Kent, the fog became so thick he could no longer see the kerb. Mum had to get out and walk ahead of the crawling car, shining a torch so that she could keep Dad on the right side of the road. Such smogs could last for days. The most notorious one came down on 5 December 1952 and did not disperse until the 9th – nearly a week of day turned into night and a clogging and deadly pollution so palpable that, after it had gone, an oily grime was left on windows and paintwork.

Overall, across the country, as many as 12,000 are estimated to have died prematurely as a result of breathing in this muck. It took another four years for a Clean Air Act to be passed, and some years after that for the smogs to no longer clog the winter air.

SIX

the suburban home

The one thing that everyone who doesn't know about the suburbs thinks they know about the suburbs is that the houses there all have lace curtains at the windows. And they're equally sure that just behind them skulks a busybody with hands poised to twitch the curtains aside so the comings and goings of neighbours can be seen and mentally logged. It's a tired old cliché that falls at the first hurdle, one of the features of such curtains being that they don't need to be touched to get a view. Unparted, they allow the watcher to see out while simultaneously screening them from the watched. Thus, any front room is turned into a sort of bird hide.

Our road's resident observer was Mrs Pobjoy, known to Mum and Dad as Mrs Peepjoy. She lived opposite and was, for all her nosey-parkering, something of a benefactor to us. Every Friday afternoon when we were young this jolly woman, who resembled the late Queen Mother but spoke like the actress Irene Handl, would walk over the road and slide a couple of Mars bars for us under our back gate. But, when not doing this, taking her dog for a walk or making sure her husband Sid's Masonic regalia was ready for the next Lodge meeting, she was an enthusiastic noter of local activity. We never actually saw her at the window, peering through the gauze of her lace curtains, but her detailed knowledge of which tradesman went to which house, and when, rather gave her away. 'I see the collars man was late again,' she might say, or, 'There's been another delivery at number 27.' Very little escaped her. And in the 1950s and 1960s – with almost every house in the suburbs containing a housewife at home during the day, and all the regular deliverymen calling, plus Mormons and other evangelisers – there was much to monitor. (When the Holy Joes called and asked 'Does Jesus live in this house?', we were always tempted to answer, 'No. He's at number 35,' and point them in the direction of the church organist two doors down.) Pity the poor nosey-parker nowadays, with virtually everyone out at work and the only door-knockers being drivers of online shopping vans looking for somewhere to leave the absentee's purchase.

Nor, to tackle the crux of the 'lace curtains of suburbia' idea, were they ever hung at the windows of every home. Rejected by some for their bland appearance and by others for signalling a lack of fashionableness, their use has always seemed strongly related to the size of the house, being less and less common the higher up the housing ladder you go. Seemingly ubiquitous in a street of terraced houses, they peter out to rarities in avenues of double-fronted detacheds. They're a kind of privacy meter: the less secluded your property, the more likely you are to fit nets. Set back from the street up a curving gravel drive, there's not much need for the screening they offer. But if your front room is near the pavement, nets let you keep your furniture, décor and general level of tidiness to yourself. Take them away, and your front room and its contents are as available to the gaze of passers-by as a well-lit shop window.

Mum and Dad couldn't abide the things. This was partly aesthetics (not much point in having mock-Tudor leaded lights if you smothered them with nets), but was also – in the age of pea-souper fogs, near-universal cigarette and pipe smoking, and rooms heated and fugged by coal fires – simple practicality. Nets were a bit of a fag to keep clean. So rapidly would they discolour that, in the winter, it wasn't just the house-proud taking them down and washing them every few weeks or so. Thus, a second net for every window would have to be kept in reserve so it could be put up while its dirty twin was being cleaned. Some nets were straightforward affairs, with possibly a small element of self-patterning; others had considerably more to them: swirls, floral shapes and complex perforations so that they looked like giant doilies hanging above the windowsills. And then there were what Mum called 'show-off curtains', nets with sweeping swags, ruches and flounces that resembled the drapery of a sultan's seraglio. These, when visiting a new friend, were a lowering sight, an infallible sign that his mother would be far more concerned you didn't import mud into the house than with making sure you were properly lemonaded and caked.

The process by which something becomes supposedly typical of a certain kind of home, as net curtains have, defies understanding. But, like all clichés, once planted in the wider cultural mind it is almost impossible to shift. Two further examples. First, ducks on the wall: three china wildfowl, modelled in flying formation and with flat backs so they could hang flush on a wall. These were produced by the Stoke pottery firm of Beswick, and sold moderately well, but never in sufficient numbers to justify their reputation as the very symbol of suburbia. In a lifetime of living in outer London, I've yet to see these birds in their supposedly natural habitat: the wall of a semi-detached. Second, Basildon Bond writing paper, the favoured writing medium for letter-writing suburbanites at a time when, in order to communicate with suppliers of goods and services, compose complaints and keep in touch with distant relatives, you had to put pen to paper. Basildon Bond is an early example of a product being named to give it snob appeal, i.e. suggest it had more class than it actually did. It was launched under this name in 1911 after the directors of the paper firm Millington's attended a shooting party at a stately home near Reading called Basildon Park. They correctly surmised that the name would evoke in suburban minds an image of the lady of the house composing her letters while seated at a walnut-veneered bureau, with inkwell, blotter and sealing wax all to hand. These days, when shooting weekends in grand country houses no longer feature quite as much in the newspapers as they once did, 'Basildon Bond' is more likely to suggest the Essex suburb of the same name. However, metropolitans sneering at its users should know that it was the writing paper of choice for poet and roustabout Dylan Thomas, never likely to be confused with a resident of Acacia Avenue.

In the 1960s and 1970s, no sideboard or cocktail cabinet was complete without its lava lamp – a glowing glass container full of coloured water and globules of wax that, heated from the base, would rise slowly in coagulating shapes before cooling and falling to the bottom to start a shape-changed rise to the top again. Mick and I bought Mum and Dad one in 1970, and it proved so indestructible that it was still going strong when Mum moved into a nursing home more than thirty years later. Respectable owners of these lamps would have been surprised to know that their inventor, Edward Craven Walker, was a public-school-educated accountant and wartime RAF pilot, whose great passion in life was naturism and making films about nudist colonies. Members of the sort of cinema clubs where such films were shown may recall his *Eves on Skis*, featuring naked female slalomers, and his masterpiece, *Travelling Light*, showing nudist swimmers. Sales of the latter film enabled him to buy his own naturist resort, where he once caused a stir by trying to bar any nudist he regarded as overweight. He had previously run an agency which found families for the large number of young Continental women wishing to become au pairs. Young women, clothed or unclothed, were thus something of a theme in his life.

The lava lamp was a rare example of an ornament in our house. Mum and Dad were very much down on what they called knick-knacks or 'dust-collectors'. Our house always looked as if it had been visited by a very tidy burglar who'd removed everything from the shelves, mantelpieces, plate racks and sideboard tops, but left no mess. I never knew Mum or Dad to buy anything that was purely decorative. Not so Grandma Randall. She was a great believer that children should be seen and not heard, and a visit to her home meant sitting silently on poufs, keeping an ear cocked for the offer of a biscuit or bit of cake, and hoping it wouldn't be much longer before Dad rose to his feet and declared we must be going. But most of all, it meant gazing at the crowded contents of her front room. There was much to take in. Unlike our own ornamentless home, Grandma's front parlour had lots of old stuff. Against the wall facing the bay window was a large faux (at least I hope it was faux, given its subsequent fate) Queen Anne cabinet full of what I now know to be Crown Derby porcelain, the gilding on the Japanese patterned cups, saucers and plates making me wonder when I was young why Grandma, living in this small house in Wandsworth, would have gold treasures in her home. On the wall to the right, the one dividing the room from the hallway, were two other tall glazed cabinets full of more fine china, some of it the unmistakable jasperware of Wedgwood. But what kept taking the eye was the marble fireplace, so large and dominating that it would have been more in scale with a Pall Mall club than this Victorian terraced house. At the centre of its deep mantelpiece was a golden ormolu clock, and, at each end, were ebony sculptures a foot or so high of Roman charioteers.

Quite what these exotic objects were doing in the home of our lower middle-class widowed grandmother is anybody's guess. I might be able to make an educated guess at their provenance had they been passed down the generations to me, but they weren't. When Grandma died in 1964, her two children (Dad and Auntie Doris) paid – actually paid – someone to take them away. Such was often the fate of would-be heirlooms in those days before endless antiques programmes on television, and beady-eyed attitudes towards the contents of elderly relatives' homes, had sensitised people to the value of the old.

My wife, too, was deprived of her heirlooms in rather more upsetting circumstances. A grandfather clock and round Georgian dining table shone out among the utility furniture of her father's home, until, one day, two spivs 'on the knock' called at his house when he was in his 80s and gave him a few hundred pounds to take them away. Table and clock would have been smartened up, price-tagged at a minimum of four figures, and in a Bond Street saleroom within the month. What we minded was not so much the loss for ourselves as the diddling of her war hero father, who by then was no longer as sharp as he'd been in his prime.

If Mum and Dad were immune to the charms of ornamentation, they did have an occasional weakness for the furniture fads of the day. They managed to give the suburban craze for picture windows a miss, the means by which many a semi had its character surgically removed. But they succumbed to the interiors equivalent: an early 1960s fashion for boarding over feature staircases and panelled doors with slabs of hardboard. This was not a sudden enthusiasm for modernity, but because Dad decided that, if the staircase spindles and door mouldings were boxed in, Mum would have less dusting to do. Indeed she did. So did many women at that time, for boarding over stair and door panels was vigorously promoted by television's first makeover programme presenter, a man called Barry Bucknell. The nation's apprentice home improvers may not have shown quite as much keenness to follow his lead if they'd been aware that he was a conscientious objector during the war and had recently served as a Labour councillor, neither activity (or inactivity, as they would see it in the case of 1939–45) usually going down all that well in the suburbs. Maybe

Dad got wind of Mr Bucknell's antecedents, for he didn't go the whole recommended hog and cover the hardboard with Fablon, sticky-backed plastic sheets available in a wide range of unpleasant patterns. Mercifully, Mum and Dad confined Fablon to the insides of kitchen shelves.

And then there were gadgets, outstanding of which among their collection was the hostess trolley, a sort of electrically heated sideboard on wheels which enabled the dinner party giver to keep the meal hot until it was served. Made of metal, and about half the size of a real sideboard, the hostess trolley was given a veneer of dining room presentability by a wood-effect coating. It was launched in 1953 as the age of servants in even wealthy homes was coming to an end. The idea was that it would allow the preparer of the meal (presumed to be female, hence the product's sexist name) to be able to decant the food into heated compartments and so, when her guests arrived, be free to socialise rather than toil in the kitchen. It sold in fair quantities, often to couples who rather liked the idea that they were the sort of people who might throw a dinner party, even if they rarely, if ever, actually would. The hostess trolley was therefore one of those things, like fish knives or, later, fondue sets, that aspiring suburban couples bought or were given, but rarely used.

The other gadget which, in the minds of its buyers, hinted at gracious living, was the Sparklets soda syphon. This domesticated drinks carbonator came in a variety of coloured metallic finishes, and got its gas from dark grey bulbs about 6cm long which had to be loaded into the syphon's top like cartridges in a shotgun. The conventional type was tall and cylindrical, but Mum and Dad went for the spherical Globemaster, which, bulb-wise, was double-barrelled. Its ownership hinted, I suppose, that whiskies and sodas were regularly consumed on the premises, but that was not the case with us. Dad used it mainly to make himself a fizzy orange squash. He called this a 'John Collins', which, more accurately, was a cocktail created at a Mayfair hotel in Victorian times consisting of gin, lemon juice, sugar and fizz. This would not be Dad trying to sound sophisticated, something never part of his repertoire, but, more likely, using an ironic name dreamt up as an in-joke by the staunchly teetotal Randall family.

Proper cocktails took a long time to penetrate semi-detacheds, a clear example of just how long it can take for the trends and habits of chic circles to make their way out to the suburbs. They'd been all the go at smart London hotels among the bright young things of the 1920s, but it was not until the 1960s that they reached Worcester Park and its like, doing so in the form of people installing bars and cocktail cabinets in their living rooms. The people who lived opposite, the Pobjoys, were financially a cut above us: they were detached, we were semi; they foreign holidays, we a holiday camp in Somerset; he a natty sports car, we a mere saloon. And, just as we were periodically asked over the road to see a slideshow of their ventures abroad, so came an invitation to see their newly installed bar. It sat in the corner of their living room, and was chest-height, with glazed shelving that sat atop an arc of padded cream plastic studded with buttons in the manner of superior bed headboards. Behind this hung optics, and, on top of the bar, a cocktail shaker, Sparklets soda syphon, small drum of cocktail sticks, neat pile of matching coasters and other bartender's accessories. And behind it, prepared to dispense almost any drink you could think of, was its proud owner, Sid Pobjoy. 'What will you have?' he asked my parents, and Dad, happy to admire for the sake of neighbourliness but not ready to dip the Randall toes into the treacherous waters of cocktaildom, replied he'd have a bitter lemon. Mum would have had a schooner of sherry. No doubt the Pobjoys, who were nicer than this anecdote may suggest, had other friends (he was in the jewellery trade and a freemason) who were more comfortable with highballs and Manhattans.

We never had a bar installed, but later my parents did acquire a cocktail cabinet which housed glasses and the few bottles of spirits they kept. They did, however, pay some small homage to the world of the Trocadero and Savoy by buying a supply of cocktail sticks and a small tub of cherries. Always offered to visiting friends and neighbours, they found few takers. Many years later, as we cleared the house after Dad's death, the cherries were still there, sitting in their little tub, undunked in any drink. Everyone's home, when emptied after their death, betrays the fads they fell for.

If cocktails took a considerable time to reach the suburbs, it was nothing compared with the centuries that passed before wine-drinking arrived. It was certainly well into the 1970s before I knew Mum and Dad to have a bottle in the house, and then only for consumption at Christmas dinner. It would have been a Liebfraumilch, or one of the squat bottles of Mateus Rose. I subsequently took an empty bottle of the latter to Cambridge, so I could, in the absurd fashion of the time, stick a candle in it. I hoped that this, once lit, would provide an ambience ripe for seduction when I managed to persuade a girl back to my room. In the event, such was the initiate's enthusiasm for proceedings that the candle proved superfluous. I might as well have had arc lights up.

In the realm of gadgetry, my parents drew the line somewhere, and this was with a Teasmade. The device came on a tray, combining timer, alarm-clock, kettle and cups – the idea being that, if it was properly set, you would wake to a steaming hot cuppa. This seemed a lot of faff to Mum and Dad, who never saw the bedroom as a place to linger. Habitual early risers, they preferred to come down to the kitchen and sample the light of day as they made their tea. Teasmades, popular in the suburbs because they supposedly replicated the experience of waking to a frilly-aproned parlour maid setting down your Earl Grey on the bedside table, were largely killed off by the invention of fast-boiling kettles and teabags.

One of the signs, not so much of the unmodernised home as the unmodernised family, was an upright piano occupying the wall of a living room. None of the residents could play; instead, it stood there, the last remnant of a long-gone relative who, on televisionless Sunday evenings, had enough of an ear to make recognisable attempts at 'In A Monastery Garden', 'The Indian Love Song' or 'Roaming in the Gloaming'. More accomplished homespun tinklers of the ivories might even venture some Strauss or a few snippets of something like the *Warsaw Concerto*. But now – with the musical maiden aunt having played her final chord and gone to the great amateur orchestra pit in the sky – inertia, and maybe memories, kept the instrument in place against the wall, unplayed, untuned and unloved. But it was kept because, 'You never know, Moira's girl might want to learn to play', or, 'Well, its such lovely wood ...', or 'We had one of those antiques blokes round. He wanted money to take it away. Cheek.' Thus did an accessory, if not the atmosphere, of Edwardian evenings linger in 1960s suburbia.

Labour-savers came gradually, Mum and Dad never exactly pioneers when it came to domestic technology. It was not until the very late 1950s that they bought a fridge with a door as thick as a prison cell's, thus making redundant the meat safe and the bead-edged lace doily which was always draped over the milk jug and allegedly kept flies off. A spin dryer, which vibrated violently across the kitchen floor and spurted water into the sink via a swivelling arm, replaced the mangle. And an upright vacuum cleaner superseded the Ewbank carpet sweeper and a variety of cloths and dusters, all of which looked pretty similar to us but each of which, to Mum, had their own specialist task. Woe betide the boy who, on the rare occasions we could be prevailed upon to help, used the wood duster on the skirting board, or the mirror cloth on the sideboard.

By and large we didn't help, enjoying the luxury of a mother who didn't have a job and took it upon herself to do all the cooking, cleaning, clothes washing and ironing, 'otherwise it won't be done properly'. We never saw Dad do any of these things, and, with one exception, we were not expected to buck this male trend. Occasionally, when older, we would sometimes be persuaded to make a pot of tea, but I found that if a sufficient hash was made of this you weren't likely to be asked again. I once put the teapot straight onto a lit gas ring, which was a double faux pas since it was wearing its woollen tea cosy at the time. Some parents might think this indicated further practice was needed; mine thought it a reason to keep me away from anything that involved the kitchen and naked flames. The result was, until late middle age, my ignorance of any cookery skills beyond toast-making. We were brought up to believe that cooking, and anything involving cleaning and ironing clothes, was what your mother did; and, if we ever gave it any thought (which we didn't), what your wife would do when you grew up. It came as something of a shock to marry someone who was rather keen on their career and expected a certain amount of male weight-pulling in the home.

Our one regular task as boys was getting the coal in, or, in the case of the kitchen boiler, the anthracite (a compacted variety of coal that burns smokelessly). Just inside our back gate were three coal bunkers: square, concrete, 4ft high, with an opening at ground level about a foot deep which was covered by a slat. Once every few weeks, coalmen wearing back-to-front caps to stop coal dust getting down the backs of their necks would bring sacks in through the side gate and tip their contents into the tops of our bunkers. It was our job, every day or so, to take a cylindrical coal scuttle about 2ft tall, lift a bunker's slat, shovel in the fuel, and bring it indoors.

Until I was a teenager, when central heating started to become widespread, suburban homes from October to mid April were the setting for a constant battle to create, and retain, heat. The basic thermal geography inside 31 Edenfield during those months was this: in the kitchen there was a boiler which, given the smallness of the room and the cooking that took place there, was more than enough to make this by some margin the warmest part of the house. The front room, its tidiness preserved against the unlikely event of unexpected guests, invariably went fireless, leaving it freezing cold and requiring its door to be not only always shut, but various devices of felt and rubber to be applied so that as little as possible of its chilly air could escape. Our living room was at the back, and it had a real coal fire. This sounds cosy, suggesting late afternoons in January toasting muffins on a long fork. But it was not. Most of the heat escaped up the chimney, and, until the room had warmed up, to get much benefit you had to sit close enough to the flames to give your lower legs a light roasting. You were then accused of 'hogging the fire' and told to retreat to give others a go.

A constant preoccupation was draughts: the causing of them, discomfort from them, avoiding them, and the excluding of them. Of an afternoon and evening the standard procedure in winter months was that the back room, where the television and dining table lived, was heated, and the hallway was not. Thus, cold air would – given the slightest chance – migrate immediately to the comparative warmth of the back room, creating an inrush of chilliness. So the living room door was kept closed, and any opening of it by you would provoke impatient sighs from Mum and Dad, and calls, as soon as your hand went on the handle, to 'Close the door! You're causing a draught!' But tiresome as they found our comings and goings, these were nothing compared with the irritation they suffered at the behest of the less biddable forces of thermodynamics. These would exploit the tiniest gap between door and frame, whether at the top, bottom or sides; and so, October to April was a never-ending battle to achieve a seal 'twixt door, frame and floor. All kinds of devices were deployed. Stiff flaps were nailed to the inside of the door in the hope that, when it was closed, no cold air could sneak round that way. Cushioned strips were fixed to the floor to try and block the low-level route. And, just to be sure, a felt tube in the shape of a dachshund without legs was made by Mum to lie along the base of the door and give some extra protection. But it was a conflict my parents were doomed to lose. Only in the mid 1960s, when the revolution of central heating came to 31 Edenfield Gardens, were indoor temperatures equalised, and internal doors could be left ajar without fear of being ticked off.

Upstairs, there were no fireplaces, but electric convector heaters. You had to remember to turn these on half an hour or so before going to bed, otherwise you had to undress in what felt like a cold store. To warm their bed, Mum and Dad had an electric blanket (an insulated heating element sandwiched between layers of fabric), but we had hot water bottles. When the bottle was first in your bed, it was too hot for bare feet to touch, but then, as it cooled, there was this delicious period when it genuinely warmed you, before its heat gave out and, if you were still awake, you kicked it onto the floor. Mornings were a bit of a trial on frosty days. You woke to a freezing bedroom (it being unthinkable to leave the convector heater on all night) and lay there, wondering how long you could delay the terrible moment when you had to leap from the bed into the cold, dash to the plug, turn the heater on, and dive back into bed to allow the room to warm up. When it finally had, and you slid your feet into your slippers so you could walk on the cold lino floor without wincing, you would find ice on the inside of the windows thick enough to draw a face. This did not seem intolerable, or a deprivation. It was just a simple fact of life then that you had no expectation you would be comfortably warm all the time.

In the bathroom, different, non-electric arrangements applied. A bath on a winter's day required a paraffin heater to be brought in and placed near the bathroom sink. It stood about a metre tall, and, once lit, the heat from it emerged mainly through a grille of six metal bars at the top of the front. It worked well, but had to be watched. Once, after I'd got out of the bath and was drying myself with my back to the heater,

I dropped the towel. I bent down to pick it up, but was standing too close to the heater. My backside pressed against the very hot grille, and I was branded by it across my backside. For a week or so, when undressed, I looked as if I was owned by the Six Bar Ranch.

Mum and Dad holidaying in Dorset after his demob in 1947. Mum was evidently proud of the fur jacket, for the picture was taken in August.

DR (left) and Mick in the garden at Ipswich in 1952 – a tendency for me to get out of my pram evident even at that age.

Our house at 31 Edenfield in 1953. With its leaded lights, oak door, wrought-iron hinges, half-timbering, pargetting, oriel window and pebble-dashed walls at the side and rear, it had virtually a full set of Arts and Crafts embellishments.

DR and bridesmaid at the marriage of his cousin Daphne Edmondson in 1955.

DR and brother Mick, aged 4, just about to cause embarrassment at Bracklesham Bay Holiday Camp, 1956.

DR and brother Mick, aged 8, in full cowboy outfit rig in the back
garden at Edenfield in 1958.

DR and Mum in 1959, with me sporting the swimming trunks knitted by her. Already, after only a brief splash in the surf, they are beginning to sag somewhat.

Mum joins DR and Mick on a bench outside a pub in 1961, our usual perch when she and Dad stopped to refuel. It was wondering what mysterious pleasures were available inside that inspired us to open our own pub.

A rare picture of DR (left) and brother Mick fighting according to the Queensberry Rules in 1962.

Shadbolt Park Library, winter 1963, in the days when the provision of handy, local book borrowing was considered as much a municipal responsibility as the provision of drains.

Mum in the kitchen at Edenfield in 1968. Black and white photography masks the clash of the yellow sink unit and mulberry-coloured tabletop.

Mick and DR, Christmas 1969. Note the heirloom fairy lights (pre-war, according to Dad), the white plastic stone-effect fireplace surround (a typical bit of 1960s DIY) and the totally bare walls of our near-pictureless home.

Posing – very much the operative word – for a picture in the rooms of David Powell at Christ's College, Cambridge, in 1971.

The future Mrs Randall, then Pamela Cleave (centre), pictured with the runners-up at the Miss Motspur Park contest in 1972. An awkward sequel followed.

The staff of Varsity, 1972. Jeremy Paxman, front centre; DR with arms folded to the immediate left of the date; football writer Steve Tongue seated on the far left. (Varsity Publications Ltd)

DR graduating at Cambridge, June 1973.

SEVEN

smoking, drinking and suburban oddballs

The ruling odour of many homes in that era was furniture polish. In fact, if you meet someone born before 1970 and want, for scholarly or therapy purposes, to prompt memories of their childhood suburban home, squirt a can of Pledge furniture polish in their general direction. They will instantly be transported back to the times when Mum would occupy part of most days by zipping round the wooden fixtures and fittings with the Pledge, and by giving any glass surface a good rub with a cloth that had a dab of Windolene on it. These will be their madeleines, the trigger scents which will carry them back over the years to the time when homes routinely smelled of cleaning fluids. Jeyes in the toilet. Dettol in the bathroom. Pledge and Windolene everywhere else – all working hard to mask the indigenous smell of tobacco smoke, or, where the habit was not practised, the telltale nothing smell of 'actually, we don't smoke' virtue.

It is hard now to convey the extent to which most people smoked back then. It seemed almost compulsory, with the few who didn't do it regarded as being a bit priggish. To simply not like smoking was very odd. Look at any photograph of a football crowd of the time and there, jammed between most mouths, would be half a fag. In offices, men in suits, and some with jackets removed to show braces and armbands, would be smoking slightly larger, thicker cigarettes, with overflowing ashtrays on their desks. Pictures of social events, dinner-dances and the like, would show all but those waltzing (and maybe even a few of those) with white sticks in their hands. Living rooms in most homes had ashtrays on occasional tables as well as on the arms of settees and easy chairs. Table lighters, lest any guest come without a match, abounded. And no review of a new car was complete without mention of the accessibility and capacity of its several ashtrays.

There was, we could see from the vantage point of our suburb, a whole system of social semaphoring created by smoking. Men with a taste for cigarettes that were eye-wateringly strong went for untipped brands, like Capstan Full-Strength, and thought filter tips rather effete. To Mum and Dad (dedicated users of Player's Gold Leaf), untipped would have seemed a bit too cloth-cap. Besides, untipped were liable to leave your smoking hand's fingers nicotine-stained. Then there were the signals sent out by how you smoked. For most, it was the cigarette held between the end joints of your first and forefingers. This was the acceptable suburban smoking technique. The fag held in a cupped hand might be a sign of one who learned their smoking in the navy on a windswept deck, but was more associated with behind-the-bike-sheds schoolboy smokers, and, for some reason, workmen. These, owing perhaps to the shortness of their smoking breaks, often seemed to have a half-smoked fag tucked behind an ear, with the burnt end pinched off. At the other end of the smoking scale were users of cigarette holders, supposedly a sign of sophistication, but never an entirely convincing one. The holder lent an air not so much of polish and poise, but of amateurishness: apprentice smokers who still had quite a few years of their indentures to work out. And then there were the 'I do like a cigarette at Christmas and holidays' brigade, usually women, who held the fag between the tips of thumb and finger, as if it was likely to explode at any moment. Every so often they would give a tentative suck, immediately blow out the smoke, and then wave their hands at it and apologise to anyone in whose direction it went.

You might suppose that children of the era spent their childhoods coughing and choking amid the resultant fug. Not a bit of it. Smoking was grown up. Smoking was manly. Smoking was what Richard Todd, Dirk Bogarde and Roger Moore did. And besides, we actually liked the smell. When we travelled any distance in the family car – Mum and Dad in the front, puffing away, Mick and I sitting in the back – we would lean forward, the better to breathe in the baccy fumes. We must have looked like the Bisto kids. This appetite may well have been acquired shortly after our birth, in a bungalow in Ipswich in April 1951. We were told that after we'd been delivered and swaddled, the midwife sat on the edge of Mum's bed and they both had a celebratory fag. There would have been no need to fetch an ashtray: a couple were always stationed on cabinets either side of the bed.

Having been baptised so early at the font of Madame Nicotine, we grew up eager adherents. And, before we reached the age when we could try fags for ourselves (legally 16, actually about 13), there was always, each Christmas, a child's smoking set: a box with a liquorice pipe, cigarettes made of soft white candy with a red tip at the end, a pair of chocolate-flavoured cigars, and maybe a chocolate ashtray. Later sets substituted chocolate for the white candy, the toy fag being covered in allegedly edible paper. Sweet cigarettes were sold all year round, and, just like the grown-ups' ones, were endorsed by celebrities or television and film characters. While the likes of Bette Davis and Humphrey Bogart (dead at 57 from cancer of the oesophagus) promoted real cigarettes to parents, boxes of candy smokes bore the names of Laurel & Hardy, Doctor Who, The Beatles, Dixon of Dock Green, Joe 90, The Flintstones, James Bond and Superman – to us, a royal flush of celebrity smoking endorsements. Sweet cigarettes were also sold in cartons that exactly mimicked those of real American brands such as Pall Mall, Camel, Winston, Chesterfield and Marlboro. American children could also choose orange-flavoured candy cigarettes called 'Just Like Dad!' that were sold in boxes featuring a picture of a small boy looking up adoringly at his father puffing contentedly away. No surprise really that after an infancy of this, we were soon picking out the choicer and longer cigarette butts from Mum and Dad's ashtrays, stealing some book matches, and going up to the park to try grown-up smoking for ourselves. We rather liked it, and, once we'd sussed out which local shops took an indulgent view of what a 16-year-old looked like, we graduated to buying whole ones for ourselves. Park Lane was a favourite brand, not because of its flavour but because they were sold in fives. We even heard talk of a shop in Raynes Park that would sell you cigarettes in ones and twos.

Mum would have a sherry or a gin and tonic, Dad a shandy and very occasionally a sherry or G&T. But they only drank if at the golf club, staying in a hotel, or if there were visitors. They would have no more thought of having a glass of wine with a meal at home than becoming naturists. This was the norm for people of their generation and class, strong drink not then being regarded, as it was later, as something without which socialising was well-nigh impossible. There was something of a family tradition of preferring the likes of blackcurrant cordial to hooch. Dad's father and grandfather were not only teetotal (a trait I've inherited) but had both 'signed the pledge': the commitment to avoid all alcohol urged on members of the lower and middle classes by the Band of Hope, a temperance campaign started in 1855 by a Leeds Baptist minister. When I first learnt about this, I presumed that it was prompted by an earlier Randall being a martyr to the bottle, possibly my great-great-great grandfather, Frederick, a Wiltshire-born shoemaker. But signing the pledge, which seems now like a bit of ostentatious puritanism, was remarkably widespread. By 1935, the Band's pledge had been signed by no fewer than 3 million people, many of the younger ones inspired less by the joys of abstinence than the promise of the Band of Hope's famously good and well-provendered annual Whit Monday outings.

Despite our parents' moderation, pubs held a wonderful fascination for Mick and me. Cross-country journeys when we were young were sometimes broken by a stop at one. We remained outside (in the garden, or on one of the benches then common outside country pubs), and would be supplied with orangeade and crisps while Mum and Dad had a shandy or a sherry within. Few pubs then allowed children inside, part of the point of them being that they were child-free – indeed, in some areas women-free – zones. The upshot was that we grew up wondering what magical mysteries lay behind the beguiling door marked 'Saloon Bar'. Pubs exerted a pull on us that was almost gravitational. And so it was that, aged about 10, we decided to open one: a sort of speakeasy for lemonade addicts in the bicycle shed just inside the tall wooden back gate at number 31.

The bar itself we assembled from an old hot-water tank, upon which rested a few old fence timbers. It filled the doorway of the shed, and was uneven and a little wobbly. Its unsteadiness, however, served a purpose, providing no reliable support, and therefore encouragement, to those most annoying of pub patrons: bar leaners. Our young drinkers, once served, were expected to step a few feet away and imbibe by the coal bunkers. Behind the bar, we sought to create the right ambience by slicing from Dad's old *Readers' Digests*, and then pinning up, colourful full-page drinks ads, thus adding, we thought, a touch of racy sophistication to the bare wooden walls. As our customers sipped their drinks, they could gaze at the ads for lemon rum and 10-year-old malts, and imagine themselves transported to a world of lounge-lizardry. Well, they might have done had they not been drinking lemonade powder mixed with water served in plastic cups salvaged from the surrounds of a holiday camp coffee machine. Extra authenticity was added by beer mats purloined from golf clubs and other such places. We charged 1*d* a cup and there was a steady trickle of patrons, only one of whom ever complained about the taste of the sickly beverage. Food was occasionally available, Mum once making us a cherry flan to be knocked out at 2*d* a slice.

Mum and Dad thought the venture amusing and one evening pretended to be customers, bringing not only their own chairs but also, so they could have something more to their taste, a gin bottle and supply of tonic. Grandma Randall, however, the widow of the Band of Hope pledge-signer, was horrified. 'Anyone would think your father and mother lived in pubs,' she said with disgust. And, as word of the venture spread and customers grew in number, our parents became less sure about it. The denouement came when Dad returned home from work one summer's evening, bowler-hatted and briefcase-bearing, to find chalked in large letters on the back gate: 'Bar Open.' Our pub was closed forthwith.

Our spell as junior publicans may have left a longer-lasting mark than we intended. Our church's midnight Mass service on Christmas Eve was often attended by those who had spent many hours toasting the season. One year, an old customer of our pub, by now in his late teens, arrived plainly and vociferously drunk and began a loud, but essentially good-natured, heckling of the clergy. He was ejected by a churchwarden but, instead of sensibly weaving his way home, he remained outside, periodically hammering on the huge wooden doors and calling out for all to hear: 'Let me in! I'm a Christian.'

When I was older and writing for a living, I would occasionally joke that my happy childhood had robbed me of the chance to write a great novel or play. After all, if doing A-Level English had taught me anything it was that very few great works seem to have been written by happily married, buoyant types who greet each morning with a cheery whistle. Quirky genetics or a miserable and emotionally blighted childhood seemed to be what supplied the necessary creative juice, and I was sorely lacking on both scores. Of course, an absence of talent may also have had something to do with it.

But happy my upbringing was, and happy I have pretty much always remained. My great school and university chum, Lenny Hodges, was made of more complex and interesting material than me, and would, when he wanted to pull me down a peg or two, claim I was 'smug'. This was his interpretation; mine was that he was, like many a literature undergraduate, prone to overanalyse and see layers of meaning in matters that, to me, seemed pretty one-dimensional. My contentedness seemed to him positively irrational, as did what he called my bourgeois attitudes. But throughout my childhood and student days he was a richly entertaining and stimulating chum. We started primary school on the same day in 1956, went to the same grammar school (where, in the sixth form, we were a double-act of bookish pretension, scoffing at the hearty, laddish sporty types), and both went to Cambridge, he to Selwyn College, me to Clare. We remained close, and, in our second year, he directed me in a production of N.F. Simpson's *A Resounding Tinkle* in which I – lacking acting ability but not front – played the thing as if it was *Puss in Boots* rather than a leading work of the Theatre of the Absurd. Once graduated, Lenny, always far more adventurous than me, went off to Italy to teach English, while I put on a suit and began my career. We lost touch and then, about ten years later (by which time I was working for *The Observer*), he made contact and we arranged lunch.

He had always seemed someone who, as he went from school to Cambridge and thence to a roaming sort of existence, seemed increasingly to be looking for something he could never quite find. Maybe, I thought as we met, he had now found it, for the transformation in him was extraordinary. The shoulder-length hair of undergraduate times was shorn, as was the bushy hippy beard. He wore an orange top, and around his neck on a string of wooden beads was the portrait of a white-bearded Indian man. It was the Bhagwan Rajneesh, a spiritual teacher and guru, some of whose followers may have been lured in as much by the free love he advocated as any of his, to me, bogus philosophising. Lenny, the once-cynical student of English who had always ragged me for my unquestioning Christian beliefs, had become a disciple of an ocean-going charlatan dispensing trite nostrums to devotees who showed their gratitude by providing him with the money to buy ninety-three Rolls-Royces and a private jet. This bright Cambridge English graduate was now one of the carpenters at the Bhagwan's commune in Medina, Suffolk. Lenny took me to a vegan restaurant, and there, over some organic mush, I spoke in a suburban way of my work, wife, home and children, and he peppered talk of his new life with mystical observations. They might as well have been in Sanskrit for all I understood them. Educated in tandem from the ages of 5 to 22, we had ceased to share a language. We never made any attempt to contact each other again.

Lenny was an extreme example of the thoughtful child of the suburbs who defines him or herself by rejecting all they have known in their youth. Oddly, in all our thousands of chats, I never once heard him talk of any great domestic unhappiness or conflict, which, of course, is not to say it didn't happen. But his parents, pleasant people who owned large shops and lived in a detached house in Cheam, must have wondered why their only son took the path he did. There must have been times when they – about as conventionally suburban as it is possible to be – questioned if all that book learning and the hothouse of Cambridge had been entirely a good thing. But then university could have a strange, and not always expected, effect. There was one chap in our school who, having won a place at Hull University, abandoned his suburban Surrey vowels almost overnight and replaced them with those of one of Yorkshire's grittier natives. He referred to a place called 'ull, and began peppering his speech with various 'ayes' and 'ee lads'. All very disorientating for his family who, having sent their son off to a Surrey grammar school aged 11 to mix with lots of nice boys, found him at 18 transformed into one of the earthier characters from *Wuthering Heights*.

The trainee Yorkshireman was not a friend but one of those characters whose antics are recalled from schooldays, often with more clarity than those of people who actually were friends. There was Martin Sellars, a boy at our primary school who we thought of as fat, but, by today's standards, was no more than slightly overweight. But he more than passed muster as our local Billy Bunter by arriving at our 10th birthday party bearing a box of chocolates which he then took to a corner and polished off, even scoffing, we discovered to our amazement when examining the remains afterwards, the coconut ones. He later cured himself of the chocolate addiction, slimmed down, and became, I think I'm right in saying, something of a local heartthrob. There was Marion Clarkson, a girl at our primary school who featured not at all in our lives then, but, within a few years of leaving, had been transformed into a willowy vision with long straight hair. If she passed by us in the street, all conversation would cease as we stared at her sashaying form as it retreated. None of us ever plucked up the courage to speak to her. By then, she was far too obviously out of our league. And then there was a pair of ginger-haired twin girls who lived round the corner from us and who, unlike my twin and

I, were identical, and, also unlike us, carried on being dressed alike until well into their late teens. To see them walking down the street made you wonder if you had suddenly begun to suffer from double vision. Unlikely, but you never knew. They were perfectly harmless, and may well have been very pleasant, but they, perpetually the mirror image of each other, always struck me as rather unsettling. They looked, somehow, as if they had been manufactured rather than born.

Mick and I were somewhat reluctant twins. No stranger would have ever taken us even for brothers, and we were apt to be militant about having separate identities, rather than being grouped together as 'the twins'. We were only about 5 when we strenuously objected to being dressed alike, and, thankfully, Mum and Dad took the hint, and no more were we trotted out of the house and exhibited as a matching pair. After all, it had been obvious from a young age that we were very different people. Me academic, him not. Me hopeless at trying to make something, him supremely talented at it. Me a bit gormless-looking, him not. He, in moments of annoyance, called me 'Fish Face'; I retaliated by calling him 'Dimmo'. But having a twin brother gave me – for all our occasional fights over toys – a built-in, in-house playmate. He was less fortunate, it being a dreadful comment on what an inadequate sibling I was that, between the ages of about 3 to 6, my twin felt the need to have an imaginary friend. Called Wing, he apparently lived in an upstairs room of a house on the 213 bus route we took into Kingston. As the bus approached a corner in New Malden, Mick would begin to look out for Wing who, without fail, according to my brother, would be there at a window to wave to him. Wing seemed a bit useless as friends go, since he did nothing except wave, and then only when we were on that particular bus passing that particular point. He must have had a very sure grasp of the 213 bus timetable. But from Mick's point of view, inventing a friend must, in the light of my selfishness, have seemed an entirely logical move. One of my worst atrocities was one Christmas morning when we were about 8. Having opened all my presents, I crept into Mick's bedroom, unwrapped a few of his, then woke him up and told him what he'd got.

Mick suffered in other ways from having shared a womb with me. I was in the school sports team, he was on the sidelines. I went to grammar school, he to the secondary modern. Relatives and Dad's friends were not always alive to what he must have felt at the inevitable comparisons. I remember one day at Dad's golf club when someone he knew came up to us and said: 'Ah, so these are your two boys. Which is the bright one?' Dad instantly said: 'They both are.' (Mum and Dad were scrupulous in treating us alike. When I passed the 11+ I was taken to one side and told that I would not, as others would, be getting a present for passing, as this would be unfair on Mick. It was the intelligent thing to do, and, remarkably, I understood.) But Mick went into and through his teens with a show-off, fractionally older brother to endure. His reaction was to become more modest than he already was, even as my cocksureness grew. An example: one morning, when he was 16, he told Mum and Dad that he would be late home as there was something going on at the school and he had been asked to help shepherd parents from car park to hall. Late that evening, he returned. When he put his head into the living room he was wearing his raincoat, under which something bulged. 'What have got under your coat?' asked Mum suspiciously (her default tone of voice for many of the questions she put to us). Mick put his hand inside and drew out a large silver trophy. The 'do' at the school had been the Surrey Schools Debating Championship, and Mick had won. Of course, had it been me competing, I would have made sure the entire street knew about it in advance, and tickets would have been distributed. But not Mick. It was not his way, nor was it ever. And, having drawn a little apart in our late teens, once we ceased to live under the same roof we became each other's best friend. We live an hour and a half's drive from each other now, but talk on the phone pretty much every day.

Our friends bore names that fixed them as boys of a certain era as surely as if they had been date-stamped. It is said that you can get an approximate age for a hedgerow by counting the number of species growing in a 30-metre length, with each species of tree or shrub equating to a century. By a sort of parallel yardstick, people of a certain vintage used to be dateable by their Christian names. Ours was an era of Brians, Martins, Stevens, Keiths, Davids, Michaels, Grahams and Trevors; Susans, Janices, Lindas, Jackies, Helens, Pams and Barbaras. Our parents were Dereks, Ronalds, Reginalds, Wallies and Toms; Gladyses, Dorises, Dorothies, Joans, Bettys and Beryls. And our grandparents were Joes, Percies, Jacks and Samuels; Emilies, Florences and Ediths – names no contemporary of ours would conceivably be given. These days, even if the fashion for trite invented names (Sparkle, Apple, etc.) is ignored, names are no longer a guide to age. An Elsie could be a 6-year-old, or her 87-year-old great-grandmother. A Joe could be a toddler, or his great-uncle.

Our assortment of chums – the Pauls, Martins, Ians, Graemes, Keiths, Nigels and Tonies – varied according to whether we were bike-riding, campfire-making or footballing. Neither popular, nor unpopular, we never found ourselves alone when we wanted some accomplices. But, at any one time between the ages of 6 and 16, there was always a boy at school or living in our vicinity who did not have a chum. They stood out as clearly as if they had been wearing an armband with some explanatory insignia on it. The reason why they were friendless was invariably their possession of some glaring, but often relatively trivial, deviation from the norm: they had an exceptionally silly laugh; talked to themselves as they walked along the street; were a bit backward (but not enough to be in a special school); had a facial tic that was embarrassing (to you, not them; they seemingly unaware that, every few minutes, they would be vigorously gurning); or they just looked a bit odd (seriously thick spectacles or a permanently catastrophic haircut obviously done by a close, but cack-handed, relative). Sensitivity, in those days, was not our strong suit; inclusivity, a noun unknown.

They were always alone, and hung around on the edge of groups and games, trying to insinuate themselves into the circle. They were often admitted for the duration of the game, but, when it was over, and the suspension of normal relationship was at an end, everyone went off with their special friends, and the outsider was as chumless as before. And so, sooner or later, the moment that you knew would come duly arrived. They would approach you, as they had approached others before, and ask the question you most dreaded as a child: 'Will you be my friend, please?' Shame to confess, you had anticipated this so often and so well that you had a response ready. 'Well, I've got enough friends already, thank you.' But, from time to time, some flicker of human decency in my 8-year-old heart would have me mumble something that was not entirely a refusal. It might have been a dishonest (because you knew it would never lead where they wanted, but didn't have the heart to tell them) 'Maybe'; a slyly ambiguous 'Well, let's see'; or, showing that such ploys are not something only adults use, replying to the question you don't want to answer by asking another, as in: 'Oh, haven't you got any friends, then?' Even at that age you knew it would be too much to come straight out with it and ask them *why* they didn't have any friends.

With the chum-seeker I most remember, there was no need to put this insensitive question. At the age of about 9, Gregory had arrived at our school mid-term, parachuted into an unfamiliar area, miles away from where he had hitherto lived, and, for some reason, he latched onto me. Sure enough, the query came: 'Will you be my friend, please?' Since he had no apparent tics, risible defects or any other of the flaws that kept boys and girls friendless, I must have given some encouraging reply, for I was soon invited back to his house for tea. It was an odd house: a chalet-style detached home, with a thatched roof and a very long, lawned front garden behind a high hedge. It was as isolated from the rest of the houses and road as Gregory was from his new schoolfellows.

The house, it turned out, was not the strangest part of his living arrangements, for inside, the sole other occupants were not the mother and father

I expected, but his grandparents, an old boy in braces and a little bustling grey-haired woman. They could not have been more welcoming, and that was the problem. They showed me things, offered me sweets and cakes and lemonade, and were so evidently, almost desperately, eager to please. They kept on referring to me as 'Gregory's friend', and talked of future visits and trips we could all make. I left the house later on – bung-full of chocolate, cake and pop – uneasy at their and Gregory's desire for us to become inseparable. I spent the rest of that term avoiding him as best I could, and, when I could not, coming up with decreasingly plausible excuses why I could not come back for tea or have him to my house. What I was, of course, too stupid and young to realise were the probable explanations for Gregory's sudden arrival at his grandparents'. His parents had split up, or one or more had died, or was too ill to look after him – any one of which reasons would explain both his need for a friend and his grandparents' zeal to help him. Even now, nearly sixty years later, I cringe at the memory of my behaviour.

EIGHT

training for little suburban citizens

My time at Cuddington Primary School passed uneventfully, although years later Mum told me that, when I was about 9, she and Dad had been called up to see the headmistress, Miss A.R.B. Smith, about my alleged stroppiness in Mr Wiseman's class. The eminently sensible conclusion of this summit conference, according to Mum, was that any conflict between me and Mr Wiseman was a simple matter of mutual dislike – a far more level-headed verdict than would probably be reached today, when issues would be identified, behavioural specialists consulted, and, keen to justify their function, therapies prescribed. I just did not care for this jowly man, nor did he for me. Our error was to make this apparent to each other. I bear him no grudge, although I should like to record my thanks to a boy called Michael Lawes who one afternoon, after lunching too well on semolina and jam, was spectacularly sick over Mr Wiseman and his tweedy suit. No doubt his parents were summoned to see Miss Smith, and I'd like to think it would have been unanimously agreed that the combination of an excess of semolina and the sight of Mr Wiseman's bilious green suit was too much for young Michael's delicate stomach.

The rest of the teachers were pleasant and effective, and there is one to whom I owe a considerable debt: Mr Upperton, who taught me in the fourth and final years and did much to encourage my interest in history. He was not to everyone's taste: a thin-faced man with gold-rimmed glasses, dressed always in a three-piece suit. His tongue could be as sharp as his features, and he favoured the well-behaved girls over we more feral boys. But he read quality stories (*Huckleberry Finn* and the like) with a verve that captured and held our attention, and showed us slideshows of his bicyclings around Europe. And then there were his walks. The area round-about had, for all its being largely a 1930s suburb, a certain amount of history to it. Not more than a couple of miles away was the site of Henry VIII's Nonsuch Palace, the land on which Worcester Park was built had been Henry's hunting grounds, H.G. Wells had lived in The Avenue, and a hardcore of the Pre-Raphaelites rented a house in the vicinity of our school. The river nearby was the setting for John Millais's *Ophelia in the Stream*, and an old workman's hut beside it the door upon which Holman Hunt's Christ knocked in his painting *The Light of the World*. Mr Upperton told us all these things, and more, as he marched us in small groups around the district. It was the first time I was shown that real places had layers of occupation and meaning which could, with the right knowledge, be stripped back.

Mr Upperton taught me to look, and not just learn. But he did the latter well enough, too, so that when it came to the 11+ – that great pre-comprehensive school era sorting of children into grammar and secondary, sheep and goats, wheat and chaff – I was fully expected to pass. The date of the exam came and went, and I recall not a single detail of the day, the tests, nor any feelings about either. My class took the wretched exam and promptly forgot about it, until, some many weeks hence, headmistress Miss Smith walked into Mr Upperton's class and announced that she had in her hand the results of the 11+. Today, and long since, such judgements on a child and their alleged intelligence would have been sent to parents in envelopes marked 'Private and confidential'. But in the spring of 1962 they were not. Instead, Miss Smith asked the children whose names she read out to rise from their seats and stand. One by one, a name would be called and a chair would scrape back, until, in a class of thirty-odd children, about a dozen were standing. I was one, my brother was not. Miss Smith then asked those who had failed to give us a round of applause. It could scarcely have been less sensitively handled if sheep pens had been involved.

So, that September, I left behind a world of boys in short trousers and girls in checked gingham dresses, smiling teachers reading you stories, dinner ladies for the milksops to cling onto at playtime, maypole dancing, nativity plays and colouring things in. Instead, at Glyn Grammar School was a harder, gruffer, grown-up universe of masters in gowns and mortar boards, strutting 1st XI young men in prefects' garb, homework, timetables, subjects you didn't like and people shouting at you. You were 'David' no more, but 'Randall!' The teaching staff contained some terrifying items. There was 'Killer' Curtis, to small boys owner of the most fearsome falsetto in history, but, to his English sixth form, which I later joined, guide to a whole solar system of culture; Dr Death (Biology), whose face resembled a skull and who, when annoyed, which was often, randomly threw boys' pens and rulers out of his classroom's ever-open windows; Mr James, German teacher, whose sudden, shrieking shouts of anger would not have been out of place at a Nuremberg rally; Sam Saunders, the English master, whose twisting of sideburns until your eyes watered would today probably earn him a custodial sentence; and an RE master whose sudden disappearance from our lives we put down to his claim the week before to have bumped into the Virgin Mary on Epsom Common.

I was put into the third of four streams, learning German not Latin. For the next five years I performed as well as I could, which, the occasional bright moments in English and History apart, was not all that well. When it came to O levels – the exams at 16 that determined whether you made it into the sixth form – I did even worse than my record suggested I might. I failed more subjects than I passed (English among them) and just about scraped into the sixth. Quite what happened to me that summer I'm not altogether sure. There was a bad bang on the head while playing cricket, and I spent much of the holidays working at a garage, my first job of any kind. But, by the time I returned to begin my A levels (History, Literature and Economics), I was no longer a third-stream plodder, but had acquired a keen academic appetite. The change from the more-or-less rote learning of O levels to a more questioning approach in my specialist subjects suited, too. I began to shine at History under the promptings of my teacher, Mr Dorling. He was most unteacherlike in every respect save for the tweed sports jackets he wore and his efficacy at stimulating the likes of me to read and read. A bear of a man with a round, squashy face that would crumple when he chuckled (which was often), he drove a large black Jaguar, and, a bachelor, seemed to be courting the headmaster's secretary, whom he took off to lunch in his car every day. He taught me two principal things: to question evidence, and that to admit ignorance about something was the beginnings of having some knowledge of it.

At some point in my second year in the sixth, he took me into his book cupboard – an Aladdin's cave of serious history – and asked me if I had ever thought about university. I hadn't. No one in my family, nor anyone I knew, had been to university, and the idea of going to one had certainly never been discussed at home. He told me he thought that, with some serious application on my part, and some guidance from him, I might stand a chance of getting a place at Cambridge. Seeing my surprise, he suggested I share this thought with my parents. I did. My father was not impressed. 'University!' he said, saying the word as if merely pronouncing it produced a sour taste in the mouth. 'Nothing but an academic Butlin's.' He made it plain that he thought it would be a needless and probably costly three-year postponement to the serious business of making my way in the commercial world, there being, in his eyes, no other. I trooped back to school the next day and reported Dad's reaction. Mr Dorling's response was very wise. 'Your father's pretty successful in business, isn't he?' I agreed, he was. 'You know, Randall,' went on Mr Dorling, 'people who are successful often think that the road they have taken is the only road. But there are other roads.' He left it at that. In due course, I decided I wanted a crack at Cambridge. Dad saw me applying myself as I had never done before and came round to the project, and Mr Dorling began to feed me books like a drug dealer feeds an addict. In November 1969, I took the scholarship exams for Clare College, Cambridge, was interviewed, and was awarded a place.

I never went back to the school, nor saw Mr Dorling again, and it only gradually dawned on me in the years ahead that I had never thanked him for what he did to awaken some academic ambition in me. Then, many decades later, the school having run out of plausible candidates to present the prizes at speech day, they asked me. Mr Dorling was long dead, but I told the boys about him, and what he did for me, and uttered the words of thanks I should have said to his face all those years ago. I suggested to them that teachers may often seem strange items, but every so often they will say something that could change your life, and, to that extent, if no other, they might be worth listening to. Even as I spoke these words, or something like them, it occurred to me that I sounded like a propagandist who'd been thoroughly briefed and rehearsed by the headmaster. But there we are. They were my own sentiments, and I meant them.

(My grammar school – despite being state-funded and intrinsically meritocratic, with admission based solely on exam performance – was not immune to a little institutional snobbery. In those days, schools that played rugby rather than soccer definitely had more social cachet. Sure enough, towards the end of my time a new headmaster came, who, among other reforms designed to raise the tone of the place, insisted the school play the more upmarket rugby as well as the oiks' game of football. Fortunately, the school's democratic DNA asserted itself before a founder's day, boaters, wall game and fagging could be introduced.)

In our area and age, Cubs and Scouts were, if not quite compulsory, then most boys' experience, but they were not to our liking. From the start, even though we were only 8 or 9, we thought Cubs had a regimented, militaristic side we found unappetising. There was a uniform (never a plus in our view), and a hierarchy through which bigger, stronger boys rose to the top like mud gas to the surface of a pond. It was a celebration of macho, and, in between the badge-passing (all of which were practical, no badges then for reading or writing anything), the games revelled in physicality. One of them, especially, could have been designed to sort out the weedier boys, and probably was. We would all line up against a wall, and a few of the larger specimens would be selected to stand in the middle of the hall. We then had to run and dodge this picket, who used any means short of eye-gouging to bring us down. Once down, you joined the thugs in the middle. Its name was British Bulldog, the personification of numbskull bullying. Cubs, to us, was *Lord of the Flies* with woggles.

And there was, we always thought, something suspect about the leaders. Not in the sense that we thought them potential pederasts who had volunteered for the thrill of spending Thursday evenings with little boys in shorts, but in the strutting pleasure they took from being obviously in charge. Looking back, they seemed like other ranks who, once a week (and at monthly church parades when we proceeded in ragged lines up The Avenue, banners aflutter) became officers, former squaddies, ratings and ground crew who'd found a niche where they at last could be the ones saluted.

We stuck it out for a few years, probably due to its major saving grace: Sunday morning at Cheam Baths, not so much for the swimming, but the donuts afterwards. But when it was time to graduate to Scouts, we persuaded our parents – never the Baden-Powell fans other mums and dads were – that we should leave. Then, after a year or so, we joined Crusaders. This was a Bible class, which makes it sound far more pious, and far less fun, than it actually was. It met for an hour every Sunday at 3 o'clock – a few prayers and choruses (Sally Army-style happy-clappy hymns) before breaking into small discussion groups, and then a final few rallying words and songs. There was a distinctly low-church, evangelical tinge, but it was not Holy Joe. There was no suggestion we were trainee sinners who needed saving. It was all rather grown-up, and, if there were Sundays when the departing prayer seemed a long time coming, the occasional tedium was a small price to pay for what else Crusaders had to offer: football and cricket matches where enthusiasm and availability were valued more than ability (thus allowing, in this shallower pool of talent, players like myself to shine as we never did in school teams); winter evenings of table tennis, summer evenings of a game called podox (a sort of cross between cricket and rounders), camps, barbeques, fireworks evenings, carol singing round the neighbourhood in the days before Christmas, and the annual national Crusader Sports.

So, in return for an hour of very mild Christianity, Crusaders (which changed its name to Urban Saints in 2006) gave you things you actually wanted to do, in a friendly atmosphere. Much of this was to do with the leaders, who could hardly have been a greater contrast with those at Cubs. Several were prosperous (one spectacularly so, owning a house whose garden was so large a tennis court was almost lost within it – the scene of summer sports evenings and sausage cooking). But they all seemed at ease with themselves, their motive, apart from witnessing their beliefs to young lads, appearing to be no more complicated than a wish to do something good. Indeed, they exuded goodness. They had no inclination to boss us about, or be kowtowed to; and, if they harboured thoughts of brushing a hand against a youthful thigh (as such people are invariably presumed to have), they gave no sign of it. Well, except one, and he – a great shorts wearer, as I recall – was only convicted by us of looking as if he might, as opposed to actually handling the young goods.

Two leaders stood out, a pair of bachelor twins in their 30s called Pengilly – David and Philip. David was known to us all as Pengy, a toothy enthusiast in horn-rimmed glasses who drove a Dormobile, the better to cart some of us from event to event. He taught us, although we did not realise it at the time, a great lesson. Every year, at the Crusaders national athletics championships at Motspur Park, we would enter the sprints and finish among the also-rans. But the 4 x 100 yards relay we won year after year, the reason being that, for weeks before, Pengy would drill us in baton-changing so that, while the other groups' faster runners came to almost a dead stop before handing over the baton as if it were a tray of drinks, we moved seamlessly around the track, having practised setting off at just the right moment so that donor runner and recipient were at optimum speed when the thing was thrust into the hand that dangled.

Strangely, this weekly hour of religion led us, when we were about 13, to one of our few acts of genuine criminality. Crusaders, as it happened, was held in the primary school we'd once attended, and, one Sunday, four of us, motivated by nothing more malevolent than seeing if we could get away with it, thought it would be fun if we broke into the school that night. So that afternoon at Crusaders, as the leaders and attendees milled about in the main hall, I turned the key in the lock of a side-door. A few hours later, having told our parents there was extra Bible study or some such believable nonsense, we met up in the dark street outside, and, having checked the coast was clear, sneaked round the back of the school and entered via the unlocked door. It is a measure of how little we were cut out for a life of crime that, having got in and had the thrill of walking quietly through the unlit corridors, past infant paintings stuck on the wall and the little coat hooks where we had once hung our red school caps, we were at a complete loss for what to do. Vandalism or theft was out of the question (we had that much sense), and crouching in the dark and silent school proved less entertaining than we had imagined. So, leaving the place exactly as we found it, we retraced our steps, exited via our side-door, went back onto the street and began to walk in the general direction of anywhere.

We had not gone more than a few hundred yards when a police car drew up. An officer got out and said there had been reports of young lads seen entering the nearby school. 'Well, officer,' we replied in our best grammar school voices, 'we don't know if this helps, but a few moments ago we did see some rough boys.' We pointed out where we'd seen these mythical yobs, the policeman thanked us, and, rather more thoughtfully than we'd begun the evening, we made our way quickly home. Even at that age I sensed that, if we'd actually been rough boys, and answered the officer with a gruff 'Nah, mate. Seen nothin',' we may well have ended the night being questioned by juvenile offender specialists about hitherto unsolved criminal damages, break-ins and other reportable nuisances. The benefits of being truly suburban.

Another benefit was that children like us were the first generation to know television all our lives.

It may have been first broadcast in 1936, but it didn't really get going until the early 1950s, the sets being far too expensive for all but a few thousand households until then. Convention has it that the great transformer of TV ownership was the Coronation in 1953, loyal subjects rushing to buy a set so they could watch the spectacle in black and white on screens no bigger than 12 inches. Mum and Dad did indeed get a set in the spring of that year, but it was bought to watch the FA Cup Final, which turned out to be the most famous one of all: the Stanley Matthews Final when the ageing legend performed wonders in the last ten minutes to help his Blackpool come back from 3–2 down to win 4–3. A set in 1953 cost around £50 and was out of the reach of any but the comfortably off, which we just about were, and so we were the first batch of British children to be trained, in part, by what we could watch on this box in the corner.

What we sat in front of were the first ever attempts to produce something for little viewers, and, in retrospect, they have an amateurish, parlour-entertainment air. The big early success, for instance, was *Muffin the Mule*: a lady at the piano playing simple tunes so that Muffin, the very obviously stringed puppet, could dance on her instrument's veneered top. The BBC (only one channel then) soon evolved a weekday schedule for preschoolers called *Watch With Mother*. Monday was *Picture Book*, which showed infants how to make things and whose theme tune was that well-known toddler's favourite, Bach's *Orchestral Suite in B minor*. Tuesday, *Andy Pandy* (another puppet, this time in striped romper suit). Wednesday, *Bill and Ben*, more puppets, this time of men made out of flowerpots. Thursdays, *Rag, Tag, and Bobtail*, an early stop-motion animation using glove puppets of a hedgehog, mouse and rabbit. Friday, *The Woodentops*, a family of peg dolls and their equally wooden Dalmatian, Spotty Dog. Nearly all of these programmes were created by Freda Lingstrom and Maria Bird, a pair of women in their 50s who had both lost fiancés in the First World War and who lived together in a country house near Westerham in Kent. They made the puppets in a workshop in their garden, and Maria Bird narrated both *Andy Pandy* and *Bill and Ben*.

Later writers found these programmes anodyne, safe and a sort of suburban propaganda aimed at educating children to be passive and deferential – a predictable bit of communications studies nonsense. Andy Pandy and his sidekicks Teddy and Looby Loo were often low-level naughty, and Bill and Ben, who waited for the authority figure of the gardener to go for his lunch before emerging from their flowerpots to get up to their tricks, had a distinctly subversive side. And many is the parent who must have been driven to the brink of tranquilliser use by their children adopting Bill and Ben's 'Flobadobb' language, and answering the most straightforward of parental inquiries such as 'Would you like some more bread and butter, David?' with a 'Nobbolov. Ibillob sillobob, mummoblob.' Readers under 60 are advised to log onto YouTube and check out *Bill and Ben*. It is bizarre, giving the impression that the BBC had handed over the making of children's programmes to a group of magic mushroom users rather than a pair of ageing spinsters, as they actually had.

Our favourite programme, *The Adventures of Robin Hood*, was genuinely subversive, its storylines showing how a money-grubbing and cruel officialdom connived on behalf of greedy aristocrats to oppress a band of outlaws trying to help the poor and needy. What gave it an additional twist of uppitiness (although we didn't know it at the time) was the team who produced Robin's weekly half-hour adventures for commercial television: a party of American exiles who had left the US in the wake of the ultra-conservative McCarthyite witch-hunts. Led by Hannah Weinstein, an admirable left-wing New Yorker, they included several writers blacklisted by the US film industry as part of its ham-fisted efforts to purge itself of communists and their sympathisers. For the sake of possible sales of the show to the US, the likes of Oscar-winner Ring Lardner Jr (one of the famous 'Hollywood Ten') and Waldo Salt had to be credited on *Robin Hood* under pseudonyms. Both later returned to the US,

Lardner writing the screenplay for *The Cincinnati Kid* and *M*A*S*H*, and Salt winning Oscars for *Coming Home* and *Midnight Cowboy*.

But, for all the sophisticated Hollywood ways of the *Robin Hood* writers, the aspect of the show which excited us was not the redistribution of wealth from the rich to the poor, fighting injustice, or the joys of being part of a commune living in the woods, but having fights with quarterstaffs and firing bows and arrows. As my brother later wrote to me:

> *The Adventures of Robin Hood* changed our play overnight. Fencing poles became our quarterstaffs, and, after a period of experimentation with elm branches 'borrowed' from trees in Shadbolt Park, we found that the canes supporting Dad's peas and runner beans made serviceable bows and arrows. Our bowyer and fletcher skills increased quickly, 3-inch nails were fixed to arrows, and the bows became more powerful and deadly. The opening sequence of *Robin Hood* showed Robin firing an arrow, followed by a whooshing sound, and then a thump and twang as it embedded itself in an oak tree. We had no oak, so the prize pear tree in 31 Edenfield's back garden became our Sherwood tree, and was used for daily target practice. This was a mistake. Sooner or later Dad was bound to wonder why that year's crop of pears wasn't up to snuff, and, on examining the trunk, he found it to be severely holed.

He summoned us before him, and we knew we were in trouble as we saw the teeth marks in his bottom lip, a sign that he was very angry. As a punishment for damaging the tree he demanded the weapons were brought before him, and he ceremoniously broke every bow and arrow over his knee and threw them in the dustbin. Some weeks later, a period of strong windy weather flattened the peas and beans. A dismayed Dad inspected the carnage and noticed the lack of cane supports. We were again summoned before him, but didn't dare tell him that he himself had broken the canes and thrown them away.

What he did not do was raise a hand to us. Smacking, and corporal punishment in schools and elsewhere, was not illegal in the 1950s and '60s, nor even frowned upon. It was, instead, positively encouraged, being thought therapeutic for both punisher and punishee. Our parents were not great ones for smacking, and certainly would have regarded anything involving beating, belts, canes, etc. as a mark of failure on their part. Dad certainly had no need to smack. His voice, raised suddenly in temper, and the way (like his mother) he rolled his lips inward when he was angry, as if he were trying to keep down some foul medicine, were both enough to bring us apologetically to heel. Little things seemed to provoke him more than big. If you tripped over his foot while he dozed in an armchair or watched his beloved cricket on television, he could erupt. But put a football through the garage window, showering the bonnet of his new Wolseley 16/60 with broken glass, which I did once, and he was apt to say when told: 'Ah, well, these things happen.' He was, in short, swift to rile, and only marginally less swift to calm down and forgive.

Our mother I don't think I ever saw in full temper. She would get irked, rather than angry. When we wronged, despairingly irritated rather than furious was her default manner, her usual punishment being to withdraw treats rather than lash out. I'm told that smacks across the backs of the legs were administered when we were very young, but, as we grew bigger, her preferred implement was not her hand but a wooden spoon, rapped with emphasis but no great force across our forearms or knuckles. It stung, but did not do lasting damage, and would not, I think, have been much of a deterrent to the serious juvenile delinquent. But then our crimes – or, at least, those that were discovered – were never that great: a bit of cheek here, a failure to tidy up there, some persistent bickering among ourselves. We were hardly trainee mobsters.

But then, if your parents were dedicated smackers and strappers, it would not take very much to provoke them into applying a leather slipper, or worse, to your backside, at least if the stories friends told us were true. Their parents – men and women who seemed, when we saw them in the street, to be mildness itself – were, in private, their offspring assured us, martinets ever ready to remove a belt and give their sons and daughters a good larruping. If nothing else, these yarns indicated that those who need to be most watched were not always the ones who advertised their weirdness. And being a girl seemed to be no protection against this suburban sadism; indeed, one suspects in a few cases it was all the provocation that was needed.

School was always held to be the prime arena for those who believed in the value of inflicted pain. I read countless school stories as a boy, and you didn't have to turn many pages before there was a summons to the headmaster's study for a six-of-the-best caning. But these were written in an era prior even to my own and set in boarding schools, establishments where the upper classes had outsourced the raising and disciplining of their sons to staff rooms seemingly overflowing with pederasts and sadists. I recall no punishment at my primary school harsher than a brisk slap across the legs (once administered to me for shouting out of the train window on a school trip to the country). At my grammar school, there were no beatings or canings that I remember; teachers kept control by using strong personalities, formidable tempers and sudden shouts, or the usual deterrents: lines ('Write out "I must not run down the corridor" 100 times, Randall') and detentions (being kept in for an hour or more after school).

I don't know why, for it was no great imposition really, but I lived in mortal fear of getting a detention – part and parcel, I suppose, of being such a little homebody, combined with an almost pathological need to always be in control of how I spent my time. But there was something else to it: not wanting to blot my copybook, for I was the sort of boy who affected to despise the prizes on offer at school – books at speech day, a place at Oxford or Cambridge, or being chosen as a senior prefect – while secretly hoping that I would gain them. The trick was to do so while feigning indifference, and in two out of three of the above cases, it worked. In this, I was an early devotee of the cult of the amateur: winning while not seeming to practise, succeeding despite no rehearsal, thriving despite apparently not trying, and, above all, assuming an air of not being very much bothered about the outcome either way. It sounds positively Corinthian but was, I think, a defence mechanism, a way of rationalising failure should it happen. It was, at heart, very suburban: always projecting an air of contentment and certainly not showing anything that might be construed as feelings.

NINE

suburban sundays and the mystery of girls

My parents were not in the least religious, and never attended church save for weddings and funerals. But, for reasons never disclosed – it may have been they thought we ought to be exposed to Christianity's moral teachings, simply convention, or that my parents wanted an hour or so on Sunday mornings free of children, a common arrangement, I later learned, so the weekly bout of marital sex could be performed – we were made to go to Sunday school. From the start, even at the age of 8 or 9, I objected to this, pointing out on more than one occasion that, since they didn't go to church, I didn't see why we had to. This culminated one week in my absolute, heels-dug-in refusal to go. My punishment was that I was not allowed to watch that Sunday's episode of *Robin Hood*, a deprivation so great that, even now, I can see myself waiting in the hall outside the living room door for the title music to finish so I would be allowed back in.

Until the 1980s, Sunday was a uniformly muted day, even for the irreligious, which was most people. We knew almost no one who was a regular at church, synagogue or chapel (Muslims and mosques were unknown in our area and thought almost impossibly exotic). Newsagents were open Sunday mornings for the papers, pubs unlocked their doors for a couple of hours at lunchtimes, and for slightly longer again in the evening, but such were trading laws at the time that no other shops or places that sold things were in business on the seventh day. Professional sport did not happen on a Sunday, many places of entertainment were firmly shuttered, and it was, in that sense, a day of rest as described, indeed prescribed, in the Bible.

In the suburbs, the trading laws were supplemented by an unofficial set of conventions that further restricted what you could do. On the suburban Sunday, you could saw, but not hammer; raise a frame for runner beans, but not your voice. Bonfires were for Saturdays, and certainly not for Mondays, which was universally recognised as washday. We children could play in the garden, but not outside the house or in the park. Any request to do so was met with refusal. 'You can't. It's Sunday.' It remained a day of rest, with very little happening outside the family until well into the less buttoned-up Sixties and beyond. Indeed, it wasn't until 1994, with the repeal of strict Sunday trading laws, that any retailers apart from corner shops, chemists and garden centres were able to open.

It will say much to later generations that, for people of my vintage, one of the highlights of the suburban Sunday was listening to the radio. This was the big family set, not much smaller than a modern microwave oven, encased in wood or brown Bakelite and plugged into the mains. The most popular programme was *Hancock's Half-Hour* starring Tony Hancock. In 1958 it broadcast an episode, excerpts of which are still used to define the tedium of the do-nothing Sunday. It opens with Hancock just sighing and periodically blowing out his cheeks in exasperation: 'Dear oh dear ... oh deary me ... oh dear,' before adding: 'I hate Sundays ... nowhere to go, nothing to do.' It brought the house down, such a chord did it strike with people who, once a week, endured a day when almost everything was shut.

The idea of Sundays being kept sacrosanct when only a tiny minority of people still went to church might seem puzzling. But tradition died hard then, and the forces that protected it were strong, the Church, Parliament and trade unions often combining to make sure that very few people were obliged to work that day. Not to be underestimated was the fact that, in the suburbs at least, a lot of folk rather enjoyed a day without, as later became the case, a multitude of leisure and shopping opportunities to be attended and paid for. The fear of missing something (an event, a show, a bargain) didn't apply because there was nothing very much to miss.

And then there was the ever-vigilant agitation to keep Sunday as dull as ditch water by the 'Lord's' Day Observance Society, a Sabbatarian organisation founded in 1831 to prevent almost anything, save for church attendance, from occurring on the seventh day. By the 1950s it was still campaigning against Sunday pleasure – garden openings, concerts, dances, etc. – but was already regarded as a body of eccentrics, not much more rational than the religious cranks who paraded down shopping streets with sandwich boards reading 'Prepare to Meet Thy Doom'. That the Society still had leverage was due to that curious law of pressure groups which states that they can, if sufficiently noisy and annoyingly persistent, wield influence far beyond their numerical strength. (Today, the 'Lord's' Day Observance Society has conformed to that other law of pressure groups by changing its name from something describing its aims perfectly to a word or phrase which means almost nothing, in its case 'One Day'.)

And so, on the suburban Sunday, decorum, restraint and widespread tedium reigned. In our family, it was a day for pottering about garden or house, visiting relatives, or going for lunch or tea to Surbiton Golf Club, which Dad had joined when he was too old for cricket. (He had been a spin bowler of some ability, playing in the Surrey Championship for Malden Wanderers, and was able in time to amend his off-drive into a passable imitation of a golf swing.) Surbiton Golf Club was actually located in Claygate, near Esher, but its atmosphere was perfectly matched to the suburb whose name it bore, which, along with Pinner in Middlesex and Purley in Surrey, was to become a by-word for suburbanism – one of those places the sound of whose very name is guaranteed to raise at least a smirk, if not a chuckle. Surbiton Golf Club may not have been impossibly posh, nor followed the unofficial no-Jews rule that some clubs did then, but it nevertheless felt it had to draw the social line somewhere. And it drew it at what its committee thought of as proper elocution. You could be worth millions and drive a Bentley, but if you dropped aitches, or had anything more than a hint of Cockney pronunciation, you wouldn't have even got on the waiting list. If your speech did pass muster at the interview, and you could knock a ball around the course without causing undue delay to those playing behind, or injury to those ahead, you would get on the list. And then, in time, you'd be admitted to a club where jackets and ties were required at all times and in all parts of the clubhouse; tea was neat little sandwiches and a plate of fancies; and women were, high days and functions apart, confined to a small snug. There was also a strip of lino about a yard or so wide around the bar which women were not allowed to step on and so order drinks. When my father became club captain in 1975, he pushed through the abolition of these gender restrictions, earning him this rebuke from one of the more vociferous old stagers: 'You're nothing but a communist! Let women all over the clubhouse and the next thing you know they'll be wanting doilies round the holes!'

Thus were our Sundays spent immersed in these socially narrow secular enclaves, my parents indifferent to anything you might call 'higher things'. Not only did they never go to church, but I never heard them express an opinion about religion or anything filed in that tricky box marked 'spiritual'. They didn't even take the option many families did, which was to reduce the great questions of life and death to sentimental comments about how Uncle Dennis was looking down on them and chuckling, or, when Grandma Randall died, how she would now be reunited with her Alfred. (Such remarks always seemed a bit of a cop-out, since quite where Alfred and his Jessie were supposed to now be, or how they were going to occupy eternity when they'd not had much more than thirty mortal years together, was never really gone into.) But at least such comments would have been an acknowledgement that the issues existed. Not so my folks. If they had any thoughts about 'God,' or the prospect of an afterlife, they never shared them with me. And, sensing that, if I was going to explore these topics, home was not the place to start, I played my part by never raising them with Mum or Dad either.

So it was a bit of a turn-up when I began going to the parish church of St Mary's, Cuddington, when I was about 15. My faith seemed real enough at the time (it wore off by 20), but the lure of church had more, I suspect, to do with seeing, and perhaps even engaging with, the girls who also attended. Only later did it strike me that vicars and curates the world over must be well aware that the religious enthusiasms which grip teenagers are strongly related to hormones and an unsuccessful – unstarted, in my case – love life. It wasn't salvation or redemption I wanted, but a girlfriend. Church attendance was more a matter of running a prospecting eye over the young female worshippers than observing any devotions. It wasn't really lust, and I don't think I ever soiled the services by mentally undressing the girls from their best frocks and blouses as they joined in the hymn singing. It was more a yearning for a girl to be with and whose hand I could hold in that teenaged, proprietorial way. I had only the dimmest idea of what was supposed to occur beyond the kissing stage, and I don't recall that featuring much in my ambitions. It was more having someone to moon over.

Soon enough I had seen her, a girl of what seemed to me unblemished perfection. She was, in Dickensian terms, my Estella. And she proved even more unattainable for me than Miss Havisham's niece did for Pip. Her name, and I apologise to her if by chance she should read these words, was Paula, and she had high cheekbones, a mew of a mouth and dark hair worn in a bob. I gazed at her across the pews, dithered at the end of the service so I could walk in her wake, and pined for her as a little dog does when first taken away from its mother. It was, in this and every sense, puppy love. There was madness here. When we went to Dad's golf club, the route took us past her school, and even this gave me a frisson. I would turn my head to its entrance and, despite it being midday on a Sunday, hope against hope that she had attended some extracurricular weekend activity and I might catch a glimpse of her coming or going. I would take long detouring routes home (she lived at least a mile away), so that I could walk by her house, slowing my pace as I approached to prolong the time it took to dawdle past. My idea was that she might, as I ambled along, look up from what she was doing, glance out of the window, and rush out of the door to greet me. It never occurred to me that, having sensed my laser stares at her in church, she would, had she actually seen my furtive parade, have made sure she kept herself well out of sight.

I was too dim and inexperienced even to realise that my near-zero chances took a fatal knock after what happened when, one Sunday, I managed to finagle my way into sitting next to her in church. In her understandable nervousness at having this boy panting by her side rather than gawping at her from a safe distance, she knocked her hymn book off the little shelf in front of us and into the pew in front. My chivalrous instinct aroused, I immediately stood and stretched over the pew to retrieve her book. Unfortunately, the pressure of the pew back on my stomach caused me to loudly break wind. Flushing purple with embarrassment, I handed her the hymn book and sat squirming with shame throughout the service. But, since deluding oneself was the chief characteristic of the smitten, I had soon replayed the incident in my head enough times to convince myself that she would, of course, regard the incident as too indelicate to commit to memory.

And so I went on, lovelorn and daydreaming that one day she would allow me to fold her in my arms, take her hand, and go for long slow-motion walks through soft-focus fields. The fantasy of her was so important and delicious (you could fool yourself, as you drifted off to sleep, that success was at hand), that doing nothing to destroy it became, in a way, the main object. Even at this age (I would have been about 16) I knew that, so long as I did not declare my interest and ask her out, there was no chance of rejection and the bursting of my bubbles of hope. But, eventually, and I cannot now remember how, my intentions were made plain. The answer was no. It would have been done gently (she was not proud or cold, as Dickens's Estella was), but it was non-negotiable. I accepted it, and never walked slowly past her house again. I learned then that I had no appetite for persisting with advances once the first had been spurned. As soon as it was clear feelings were not returned, I was off. None of that 'well maybe we could just be friends and see how it goes'. The slightest suggestion of disinterest was enough for me to take my sheep's eyes elsewhere.

Girls, when we were very young, were very rarely on the agenda. We were two boys, our cousins were boys (albeit considerably older), and only one neighbour had a daughter. Until we realised that girls had a significance beyond playing skipping games and telling teachers about the unpleasant things we boys had been up to, they were peripheral creatures in skirts and long hair, and so unlikely candidates to be playmates. When I first went to primary school, however, one of them was briefly my friend. I recall not much more than us linking arms and skipping down the road in our gumboots, and then visiting her home for tea. Her name was Hanna Lawrence, and the surname may have been a recent invention (or Anglicisation), her parents being what I took to be German émigrés. This was the mid 1950s, a mere ten years after the end of the Second World War, and, whatever brought them here, it, and the subsequent settling in, would have been far from easy. They were not, after all, likely to be mistaken for long-term Worcester Park natives. Her father was almost a stereotype of a Germanic scientist or engineer: darkly suited, thick horn-rimmed glasses, a marked accent and lots of intimidating books on his shelves. Her mother was altogether less frightening: slim, pretty, fair-haired – Teutonic in the best sense. She would have worn a dirndl well, although, wisely, she didn't. She did, however, bake strange foreign cakes that were only very distantly related to those I had hitherto known, a third cousin four times removed (at the very least!) of the rock buns I was used to.

It may have been the odd things I was offered at teatime which put paid to the friendship with Hanna, although I suspect it was simply reverting to our own genders for chums.

Just before completing this book, I made contact with Hanna for the first time in nearly sixty years. She told me her father had come to Britain aged 18 in 1936, was fostered with a family in Belfast, went to university, and then, as a native of a hostile power, was interned in Crumlin Road Gaol. He joined the British Army and was advised, lest he be captured, to Anglicise his name. So, Ludwig Levin became Leonard Lawrence, and it was in this new identity that he became a tank commander with the 8th King's Royal Irish Hussars. He later worked at the Nuremberg War Crimes Trials, where he met his future wife, a secretary of 18 called Elfrieda Popp. He returned with his bride to Britain in 1948, and here they raised their daughters. Hanna said: 'As a young child I already knew that our normal was not the same as other people's, especially when it came to food, and that has stayed with me, of course. I can remember name-calling in the playground at primary school, and being greeted with a Heil Hitler salute, but not understanding much about it except that it was connected to having German parents.' Hanna later went to Oxford and taught languages in schools. She now lives in a self-build community in Telford, has three grandchildren, and leads singing groups.

Until the first stirrings of puberty, my brief friendship with Hanna was about the size of it as far as contact with girls was concerned. They were there at school, the Lesleys, Lindas, Helens, Susans and Jackies. But they were not talked about by us boys, much less played with. The exception to this indifference, mainly because she could not on any level be ignored, was a tall, big-boned girl called, well, let's say she was called Janice. She was often to be seen at playtime talking to herself by the fence, but would occasionally burst into alarming life, her outsized body charging lopsidedly about the place. Such were her size and unpredictable movements that the effect of this was like that of a runaway horse, scattering the playing children in all directions. What a girl of such obviously special needs was doing in our school was a mystery known only to Surrey County Council's education department. For all that, and the strange noises she made, she wasn't bullied or picked on.

Our boys' world went on, so that when the first stirrings of puberty prompted an interest in girls, they were as mysterious to us as Amazonian tribespeople. Rather more so, in fact, since the *National Geographic* magazine – available in all good public libraries – published photographs of near-naked Brazilian rainforest folk, ostensibly to illustrate articles on anthropology, but in reality for the benefit of sisterless boys. Thus we got the general idea of what female breasts looked like; but, as to what lay beneath the loincloths, we could only speculate. Girlie magazines were slow to arrive in our lives, and, when they did, were not very helpful. *Parade, Reveille* and *Tit-Bits* (whose title promised so much yet delivered so little) all published pictures of topless models, but, invariably, the airbrush artist had been at work, his or her handiwork depriving us of the detail we were after, the unknown reality hidden behind a blurry continuation of featureless flesh. The naturist magazine *Health & Efficiency* was, in a way, of even less assistance. Ostensibly the handbook of the let-it-all-hang-out classes, the free-spirited women pictured on its pages seemed always to be sitting down, walking away from the camera, standing side-on, posed beside a man with a table-tennis bat held at a low angle, or, if they were full-frontal, photographed from such a distance that not even a magnifying glass brought enlightenment. God knows we tried.

And so the precise layout of the female body (never mind the plumbing that lay behind it – sex education then being unknown) remained a mystery until more explicit girlie mags came along. We didn't buy them, lacking both the cash and the bravado, but occasionally a few pages of one would be found in the woods and passed round for eager study like some map of buried treasure (which, in a way, it was). Occasionally, when I was on the cusp of puberty and we came across some girls playing nearby, I would entertain the thought that one might smile, beckon me into the bushes and undress so I could look and learn and solve the riddle. The idea may have been planted by an incident towards the end of our primary school days when, during a summer's lunch break, a boy called Alan Holliday and two girls took themselves off to the bushes at the top of the playing field, and showed themselves to each other. They were caught by a dinner lady, and a considerable kerfuffle followed involving parents being summoned, much tut-tutting and some absurd warnings, including one from a teacher who warned us of the danger of 'dirty little girls'. We should be so lucky, we thought.

The only time anything remotely like this happened to me was when I was about 10 and playing football in our park. A girl about the same age had stood on one of the swings, lifted her dress, lowered her knickers, and shouted an invitation to all present to have a look. Despite my curiosity in such matters, I gave no more than the swiftest of glances and carried on with our game, feeling, I recall, more embarrassed for her than interested in what she had to show. She apparently gave these impromptu demonstrations on a regular basis. She would now be in her late 60s and has, presumably, outgrown the habit, if only for the sake of her grandchildren.

When I was 14 or so, I started meeting a girl in the park. I'd seen her, admired her, and learned that, if I hung around a certain bench about an hour before sunset, along she would come with her little terrier dog. She had dark hair, always wore a crystal pendant round her neck, and was as pretty as a picture. Unfortunately, like many pictures, she was also painted, and, to my parents, any girl wearing make-up at the age of 14 was plainly up to no good. Alas, I never got the chance to find out. I was betrayed by some beady-eyed neighbour who reported my twilight assignations to Mum. And so, one evening, as the girl and I sat on a park bench talking, I heard a voice, turned round, and there, bearing down on us, was Mum demanding I come home immediately. I did. Mick recalls that the following day Mum was still muttering with disgust about me 'hanging around with bits of girl', a phrase suggesting I was an old hand at this game, which was sadly far from the case. I was barred from the park for a week or so; harsh treatment, I thought, for encounters that had not even got to the stage of hand-holding. The next time I saw my little crystal pendant wearer, another boy was beside her on the bench.

And so, being at an all-boys school, having no sister to bring comely friends home, and not being – whatever Mum thought – an experienced schmoozer of local girls, I did what millions of teenage boys did in the suburbs: nothing. I hankered for a girlfriend, but, in the absence of contact with any potential candidates, could only look and wonder. Only when I joined a youth club at our church did the matter cease to be an idle dream and become instead a theoretical possibility. A fear of being turned down kept it theoretical, and so, for a year or so at least, my experience of girls was confined to those toe-curling occasions when you'd been 'fixed up' by a more outgoing friend. These were not dates, as any normal person would understand them, since they involved no trip to the cinema, no appearance at dance or disco, nor anything you might construe as an outing. They were instead a meeting at some prearranged point and time of two girls and two boys, a rapid pairing off of your confident friend with 'his' girl, and you and her friend stuck with each other for the evening.

These coincidings of two gauche teens always seemed to take place after dark. You sat on a park bench, making small talk about records, parents, brothers or sisters (but never school), and listening, during the lulls in your conversation, to the giggles from the other pair sitting nearby. Eventually you would summon the nerve to slip an arm around her shoulders, and depending on whether she flinched or not, might even venture a kiss on her cheek. Sometimes she reciprocated, sometimes not; but the meetings, as far as I can recall, were rarely repeated with the same girl. They were, in all senses, blind dates, and, curiously, the most successful was the blindest of the lot. Three or four of us arrived at the home of a girl I did not know. We were let in, and found the rooms in darkness but plentifully inhabited by several of the resident girl's friends. I was directed to take my place beside a girl sitting on the floor who, as far as I could tell in the feeble candlelight, was blond and buxom. For some reason we clicked immediately and spent an evening fumbling, talking and snogging. Strange, but I didn't try to arrange a further meeting with her before I left. Silly, because I had caught no more than the odd sideways glimpse of her face by the glow of a guttering candle and, had I bumped into her in daylight, would only have been able to recognise her by touch. And so, faced with this impracticality, that was rather that.

Travelling hopefully, but rarely with arrival at any physical destination with girls, seemed to be our lot. But we remained optimists. At the small, family-owned holiday camp we went to for many years in the 1960s, for instance, the noticeboard was essential reading material as soon as we arrived on a Saturday. It contained all kinds of useful intelligence (times of church services, chemists' rota, etc.), but for Mick and me it also had the list of fellow campers that week. Here we could eagerly scan the names for any Misses on the list. Unaccompanied ones were rejected as probably being aged spinsters; it was the ones in parties that also included a Mr and Mrs of the same name that we were interested in. How often would we note, with rising expectation, that such a pair of Misses had been assigned to an adjoining chalet, only to see, when they arrived, that they were twin girls of no more than 10. In the end, my brother – better looking than me – was the first to show success with girls. It was, in terms of sexual adventure, small beer, but he, like all of us, sallied forth with hope. One year in our late teens, he and a friend took their first package holiday to some Mediterranean resort. Before leaving, they thought they'd better equip themselves in case they met a couple of obliging females, and went to a chemist's shop to buy condoms. Mick's friend stepped forward, cleared his throat, and asked for two dozen Durex. 'What are you two, then,' laughed the man behind the counter, 'a couple of hygienic wankers?'

In the end, proper girlfriends of varying degrees of seriousness came and went (most of their own choosing), until I met my wife in circumstances already described. But a certain suburban naivety with women persisted. In 1992, I flew to Moscow to discuss the possibility of taking a short break from *The Observer* to give a month of seminars to young Russian journalists emerging blinking into what we all wrongly thought was lasting daylight after the fall of the Communist Party. The venture was funded by what was then known as the European Community, and the organisers booked me into the Rossiya Hotel, the monster billet next to Red Square where they built 4,000 rooms and couldn't get a single one right. Outside the window was St Basil's Cathedral but inside was where the prayers were needed: a fridge that didn't work, a television with no way of connecting it to the electricity supply, and a sink with no plug. The lack of working fridge and television I could live with, but not the plugless sink. I rang reception (a vast area where men with thick necks and leather coats perpetually milled about to no apparent hotel-like purpose), but could not make myself heard, let alone understood. Maybe the matronly looking female sitting at a desk at the end of my corridor could help.

Swiftly establishing that we shared no common language, I mimed. With the finger and thumb of one hand I made a passable impersonation of a plughole, and, with a finger of the other, I created a plug, demonstrating how it would fit into the finger-and-thumb plughole – a mime, I later realised, open to misinterpretation. By the time I went to bed, at around 11 p.m., no plug had been delivered, but, unknown to me, other arrangements were being made. Soon, the bedside phone rang. 'You want massage?' a girl asked. 'No,' I replied, 'I want a plug.' 'Okay,' she said. Moments later there was a knock at my door. A girl, possibly my caller, stood there. She was no more than 20, dressed for a nightclub, and clearly nothing to do with bathroom fittings. We soon learnt we were of no use to each other. But word was not shared with her fellow artistes. For the next two hours they rang or knocked at regular intervals. Sleep was only possible hours after the last of them had given me up as a bad job. The next day, I did the uptight Englishman abroad act and told my hosts that unless I was found a hotel free from such interruptions, I would be off to the airport. I was transferred to the ludicrously glitzy Radisson, a hotel with a shopping mall where $2,000 handbags were for sale, but not, as far as I could tell, young women. It had taken me until my 40s to learn that sometimes it pays to come over a bit hoity-toity.

TEN

the great
suburban
outdoors

Worcester Park was not quite on the very edge of outer London, but if you left our house and walked half a mile in a north-westerly direction, there were fields, woods, thickets and a river: a genuine wilderness not more than ten minutes from our semi.

You walked up our road, passed the elms that bordered our park until Dutch disease killed them in the early 1970s, diagonally crossed its field where we footballed, turned right at the drinking fountain and cattle trough (a reminder of the area's agricultural past), went 150 yards along Salisbury Road, took a left turn into The Avenue and carried on the short way to the church past the forbidding-looking convent with its nuns and grounds full of statues. You then came to a rough, rutted unadopted road, and about 100 yards of that brought you to the ridge above our boyhood paradise. You entered on one of the many paths worn through the scrub and trees, and, after a few dozen yards, came to a couple of fallen trees where we could always find stag beetles in the summer. Stand by them, and you looked down on a sloping rough pasture about 100 yards square, quartered by mud paths. On the left were bushes bordering the untarmacadamed Grafton Road; on the right was a thick miniature forest of short, thorny trees where dirty old men were said to lurk, and, at the bottom, lay a large wood.

In it were marvellous things for boys: the foundations and a few scraps of wall of a ruined great house, a swamp that was all that was left of its lake, the remains of a balustraded bridge, and other strange remnants, including a brick igloo-like structure we later learned was the ice-house to the house, now reduced to stony outlines amid the bushes and trees. And beyond all this were a road, more scrub, and then a river 10 yards across and no more than a foot or so deep in summer. The Hogsmill was once the power for gunpowder mills and the setting for Pre-Raphaelite paintings, but to us it was a waterway of sticklebacks and bullheads whose surface was regularly cut by the V-shaped wakes of water voles. If you were inventing the location for a childhood of fun, exploration, some casual fire-lighting, apprentice vandalism and a little mild risk, all free of the attention of adults, you wouldn't dare come up with the cocktail of possibilities we had just a short walk from our suburban home.

Our inadvertent benefactors, though we didn't know it until decades later, were a family of misfits who had lived for nearly seventy years in the eighteenth-century house and grounds now eaten up by our woods. They came to live here in 1875: Portia Wheeler, the recently widowed Italian-born wife of a wealthy merchant, and the unmarried half of her sixteen children. None of these eight ever did marry, and one of them, the eldest daughter Portia, apparently took to her bed after a disappointment in love and, Miss Havisham-style, never re-emerged. The rest lived a reclusive and comfortable life in the house of fifteen bedrooms, four reception rooms, billiard room and all the usual domestic offices, their whims and necessities catered for by six servants. In 1901, by which time the mother was long gone, and Portia the younger had only a few more years left to sulk in her bed, the Wheelers in residence were outnumbered by the servants. There was no shortage of work for them, for beside the rooms already mentioned there were, according to the 1871 sales prospectus for the property:

> Stabling for six horses, coach-houses, laundry, with room over, gardener's cottage and two other modern cottages ... lawn, Italian garden sloping to ornamental running water, croquet lawn surrounded by timber trees and shrubs, secluded walks, rose garden, vinery, orchard-house, two kitchen gardens (one walled), melon ground, cow-house, plantation and undulating park lands.

The last Wheeler, Laura, moved out in 1938, leaving the place empty. It was hit by a wartime incendiary bomb, what was left burnt to the ground in 1948, and local scavengers and builders moved in to plunder the rubble.

A decade and a half later we came on the scene, the site already largely reclaimed by trees, plants, brambles and scrub. We knew nothing of the Wheelers, but knew a great house had once stood here, and so, when we tired of racing round the cycle tracks we made through the woods, and throwing bricks into the duckweed-covered swamp, we could dig with an old iron bar into the foundations still just about visible at the surface and hope, for half an afternoon, we might find treasure. Or we might scrabble in the earth-clogged old ice-house, unsure of what we might uncover, but certain, for half an hour or so, it would be something. It never was, and so we would use some more old bricks to make a camp, not because we wanted one but because a camp was an excuse for a campfire.

Fires fascinated us, and we often stole book matches from Mum's handbag so we could have one in the woods. We also nicked potatoes to cook, although we were far better at building and maintaining a fire than judging how long it would take to bake a spud. The woods were full of combustible timber, and it was never long before we had a cheery blaze going. Our fires rarely got out of control, but, when they did, we regarded the occasion as a sort of test of character for whoever was with us. One boy failed spectacularly, wailing and hopping agitatedly from foot to foot just because our cheery little fire had reached, and was busy consuming, a nearby bush. (I was never entirely to be trusted where open-air fires were concerned. I would often light a small, illicit one at the end of our garden, where the place for bonfires was behind a metre-high box hedge. One afternoon I'd got a small secret fire going when

I was called in to tea. I left it smouldering. A little while later, as we sat at our sandwiches and cake by the table in the back room, I saw through the window that my fire had got rather ambitious. Its flames were not only leaping up above the hedge but had also begun to consume the nearby fence and were threatening a small shed. I hesitated no more than a minute or two before pointing this out. My parents dashed into the back garden, saw how bad things were, alerted the family next door, and their sons formed a human chain to convey buckets of water to the scene. Amid much shouting, the flames were doused. Mum and Dad went to their graves unaware of the cause of this fire.)

The great thing about the woods was that they seemed to be, by some unspoken edict, reserved for boys, and the occasional girls who had early on absorbed the suburban knack of rubbing along without any undue ugliness. There were no gangs eager to pick a fight, steal your bike or make a passing threat. Nor, for some reason, was it used much by dog walkers. So you could play in the woods secure in the knowledge that at no point was some slavering Rottweiler about to bound up to you, trailing in its wake an owner calling futilely: 'Satan! Satan! Come here!' Besides, collie dogs, poodles and spaniels were more in fashion then, and not the breeds with jaws strong enough to kill a child now preferred by the shaven-headed classes and others in need of aggressive accessories. How many children, one wonders, have gone to their graves with the last words they heard: 'It's all right, he's only playing.'

As you might guess, we were not dog-owners. Too much bother, would be Mum and Dad's general take on the issue, what with walks, kennels during holidays, training, trips to the vets, etc. Nor did my brother or I hanker for pets. A couple of girlfriends had dogs, which meant, in the first flush of the relationship, affecting a fondness for the things. But my patience with being drooled on, barked at and dragged along some country lane soon wore thin. It never took long for me to want to take it for a walk along the top of a sheer cliff and throw a fetching-stick seawards. Cats, I later came to feel, were different. They were selfish bastards, but they were *your* selfish bastards.

And so down at the woods, untroubled by dogs, and unscolded by the passing grown-ups who infested the local park and so often had a chiding comment as they passed ('Do you have to kick that ball against the fence, young man?'), we could while away whole summers with what we found in the woods. Slender branches could be fashioned into staves or longbows, smaller, straighter ones into arrows, and then there were berries. A great game was to put unripe hawthorn berries into the end of a bicycle pump and, with a rapid thrust, fire them. At close range (up to about 15 yards) they had the stinging impact of a mild air gun. Our delight was to hide in bushes beside Old Malden Road's winding single carriageway and fire the hard green berries at cars and cyclists. I was made the leader of our group after I suggested that better sport could be had if we waited in bushes on a corner, because vehicles, and especially cyclists, slowed on bends. A summer cyclist wearing shorts was a particularly valued target.

But of all the found entertainments, nothing beat what we seemed to discover almost every spring or summer at the bottom of the rough pastured hill that ran down to our woods: an abandoned car. The cars of those days were infinitely more entertaining than those of today, which have everything part of an all-encompassing sealed-up body. There were bumpers to detach, metal hubcaps, badges, chrome mascots on top of radiator grilles, seats, door handles, semaphore indicators that flicked up from slots in the side, and that was before we prised open the bonnet and got to the engine. The older cars, those most likely to be dumped, had headlamps standing proud of the bodywork, positively inviting a boy with a screwdriver borrowed from his father's toolbox to detach it and carry it home. 'Where did you get that?' anxious parents would ask, fearing that their son had started going in for a little light car thievery. 'Someone's dumped a car down the woods,' we'd reply, and, thankfully, were believed. Friends would plunder away while unmechanical souls like me stood waiting for the wheels to be removed so we could roll them down the hill. I was always more interested in jemmying open the glove box, ever hopeful that documents, money, or even gloves would be found. They never were, of course – gloves, in my experience, being the very last thing you'd find in a glove box. But those cars were the best sort of toy: a found thing of adults, just waiting to be destroyed.

And when we tired of the woods, or just wanted to kick a ball about at the top of our road, there was always the playing field attached to Shadbolt Park, a small football-pitch-sized area with swings at one end and a gated entrance to the gardens and library at the other. This was the domain of the parkkeeper. Up until the 1980s, every suburban park had a parkkeeper. They would walk the grounds, picking up the odd bit of litter, reprimanding those who stood on the swings or put their feet up on the benches, and they would chat to anyone ready to stop and waste a few minutes. Ours, known to us simply as 'Parkie', was a burly man in his 60s who wore a blue boiler suit and had a toothbrush moustache. He was friendly to us kids, at that time not grounds for immediate suspicion, but his line in conversation could at times be odd. He told us once that a favourite ploy of his when growing up was to smear some mustard onto a dog's backside and watch it go mad trying to lick it off. Another party trick, he claimed, was to grab a cat, place it under his arm, put the end of its tail in his mouth, and then bite down while squeezing his arm on the animal's side, thus turning an ordinary moggy into what he said was a passable imitation of bagpipes. We didn't really believe he did these things, for he showed no sign of sadism in the course of his duties.

He was, as men of that vintage in our youth invariably were, a veteran of the First World War. He spoke a little of his time in the trenches, telling us how, when ordered to fight their way into a wood in Flanders, he and 100 or so comrades went in, but only fourteen or so emerged unscathed. It was said without rancour; it was just what men like him had to do in that turkey-shoot of a war. Retirement came to him before public spending cuts of the 1980s had a chance to summarily dispense with his services. This was the fate of so many of his kind in an era when the culling or keeping of council employees was decided purely on whether their functions, or a reductionist view of them, could be done more cheaply by private contractors. To the simplistic bean-counters, parkies' chief role seemed to be the unlocking and locking of gates at the start and end of each day plus the odd bit of litter picking. A roving gatekeeper in a van and the provision of a few more litter bins was, indeed, nominally cheaper. That the van driver and the bins could not be a constant patrolling presence, watching out for bullying, deterring lurkers and vandals, ensuring dog owners gave the beginnings of consideration to others, gritting paths in winter, exchanging cheery words with locals, getting to know the vulnerable kids, acting as a little lost property service and much else wasn't, of course, allowed to enter the equation.

With the park and the woods on our doorstep there was little need to go further afield. An occasional cycle ride to Nonsuch Park, perhaps, but until our late teens, when we discovered the pleasure of a train ride to Westhumble station and rambles round Box and Leith Hills, our play world was constantly at hand. The one exception was when, prompted probably by an article in *Boy's Own Paper*, we took up fishing. This meant a 213 bus ride to Kingston, carrying, as was our unhygienic habit, haversacks that contained both our sandwiches and maggots for bait, albeit in separate containers. A walk past Bentalls and down a scruffy industrialised road led us onto the towpath. Here, by the power station outfall whose warm waters were, we were assured, catnip to fish, we would set up for a day's angling. The way we went about it owed little to Isaac Walton, and even less to the detailed advice found on the pages of *Mr Crabtree Goes Fishing*, the bible for young anglers in those days. Mr Crabtree, in reality Bernard Venables, fishing correspondent of the *Daily Mirror* and founder of *Angling Times*, seemed in his illustrated books a dab hand at catching carp, tench, trout and other exciting and pugnacious game specimens. We, dangling maggots on a hook whose line was wound round a Woolworths reel attached to a Green Shield Stamp shop rod, went in more for the submissive small fry of bleak, gudgeon and the occasional underdeveloped roach. I soon tired of angling, and, especially, was put off by the needless cruelty with which some boys, having tried for a moment to extricate their hooks from the gasping mouths of the fish they'd caught, lost patience and simply ripped them out. Mr Crabtree would have been horrified.

The *Boy's Own Paper*, which inspired our brief angling phase, had been founded in 1878 by the Religious Tract Society. The ownership passed into other, less evangelical hands, but retained a militantly wholesome tone. Witness this exchange from the letters pages in 1951:

> Dear BOP, Most boys like to think they have a girl friend, especially the 13 to 14 year olds. I would like to see an article on how to get a girl, and when you've got her, how to keep and please her ...
> R. Wilmot (New Malden, Surrey)
>
> Editor's Reply: We will bear the suggestion for an article on how to keep a girl friend in mind! In the meantime there is an article on keeping Golden Hamsters on pages 34 and 35 of this issue.

No article on securing or keeping, let alone pleasing, a girl friend ever came. The *Boy's Own Paper*, whose contributors at one time included Arthur Conan Doyle, Jules Verne, Isaac Asimov and William Gordon Stables, inventor of the caravan, passed away peacefully, and no longer much read, in 1967.

Every summer without fail, word would circulate at some stage that there was what we called 'a dirty old man' hanging around our woods. You never met anyone who actually saw him, let alone was touched up, exposed to, or so much as approached by him. But on our Richter scale of scariness the fact that real Dirty Old Men were never proved to be operating in our area was irrelevant. The important thing was that he might be there, a possibility which added enormously to the momentary fear you felt upon hearing an unexpected sound behind you when down in the woods alone. Anything that sounded like the snap of a twig behind you, or the rustle of a bush's branches being parted, prompted immediate flight, and the telling of friends that you were sure the Dirty Old Man was back in the woods because you'd heard him, or, in your more hysterical reports, thought you might have seen him. It did not occur to us to claim we'd actually been nabbed by him, partly because even our capacity for lying never stretched that far, but mainly because we would have no idea what the mythical pervert would do once he got his hands on us. The words then used by parents and in newspaper reports to speak of what, spelled out, they would have found unspeakable was 'interfered with', an ambiguous phrase which gave we innocents no idea of what might actually take place. (It also gave rise to absurdities, the *Leeds Mercury* earning a footnote in newspaper lore by once publishing the headline: 'Girl stabbed 55 times but not interfered with.')

As time went on, and summer after summer went by without him putting in an appearance, the Dirty Old Man ceased to be frightening and became instead a figure of fun, which was how, in our comics and comedy programmes, he was always portrayed. He was shown invariably as a little balding man, similar to the weedy henpecked husband in Donald McGill's seaside postcards, who would lurk in bushes and, when a girl or woman came along, leap out and flap open his raincoat to reveal his willy. We didn't know quite what his game was, but even at that age we understood that if it was hanky-panky he was after, showing your prick to girls and women was not exactly a failsafe way to get the ball rolling. And this, given the preparations we imagined he undertook – chopping off the end of his trouser legs and sewing them to the underside of his raincoat front, choosing a good thick, thornless shrub from which to burst, wearing suitable footwear should he have to leg it, etc., etc. – was what made it funny.

Flashers were not just one of the stock characters of comics, but seemed to pop up regularly in reality as well, albeit not in our woods. Nearly every issue of local papers seemed to have a short report headed something like 'Epsom man exposed himself', giving the accused's name, age, address and occupation so that he'd be publicly shamed and forever pointed out in the street, which, the authorities knew, was the greater part of any punishment meted out. The man in the dock (and I saw enough of them as a junior court reporter) nearly always pleaded guilty, and sometimes asked for a quantity of similar offences to be taken into consideration. Occasionally they might make some brief stab at a defence. 'I was taken short, your lordships,' (over-egging the form of address to magistrates being something of a hallmark), 'and so relieved myself in this bush. Something startled me and forced me to re-emerge before I had adjusted my clothing.' It never washed with the bench, and so off the flasher trooped, guilty, fined and, only in serious cases of recidivism, sentenced to a spell in prison with the really rough boys.

As a type, as a staple of life, they seem now to have all but disappeared, although quite why is a bit of a mystery. It may be that they've simply migrated online, able now, from the comfort of their own homes, to broadcast their pricks worldwide rather than give shows to audiences of ones and twos. Technology has certainly affected voyeurs, the old-style Peeping Tom peering in at a window being replaced by the clued-up gym or hotel manager who rigs up webcams to spy on his clientele. Or perhaps sexual offences are subject to the whims of fashion, flashing now regarded in deviancy circles as old hat. It can't, after all, be the climate, warmer temperatures presumably having added a good few weeks to the indecent exposure season. (Police told a local reporter I know that weather plays quite a role in small-scale sex crimes, heavy-breathing phone calls going up in winter months, and declining as warmer days set in.) It could, of course, simply be that fewer patrolling police means Freddy Flasher has long since made off by the time one of the county's only available squad cars has turned up. Or, even more likely, the huge cuts in local paper staffs (a literal decimation in some cases) have meant that reporters are no longer on hand in the local magistrates' court to record the sad little tableau. Whatever the reason, flashers seem to have largely passed into pervert history.

Of course, one of the many things we failed to grasp about flashers, and dirty old men in general, was that, when it came to motive, sex hardly came into it. The purpose was to cause shock and fear, which they often did, despite all the apocryphal stories of spirited women who, when flashed at, gave a snort of derision and told him 'Put it away!' It was, essentially, an act of violation. For this and other reasons, girls never quite saw the funny side of the Dirty Old Man, and it was only much later, when I had girlfriends and a wife to discuss such things with, that I realised why. Every one of them had, at some stage in their life, been approached, flashed at, tampered with or violently assaulted.

So while we boys had an image of a cartoon dirty old man, risible and pathetic, theirs was of a real pervert, not necessarily old, or even dirty, but aroused and threatening. To take my wife's mercifully short encounters: the lecturer who, when she was a student nurse, cornered her in an otherwise empty classroom and forcibly pressed himself against her (she was saved by another lecturer popping his head round the door); and much later, by that time a mother of four boys, when she was helping in the kitchens of a church and an elderly volunteer suddenly grabbed her breasts from behind as she washed up, of all the unerotic occupations.

I, being a boy, and an unappetising-looking one at that, remained uninterfered with, thus depriving me – in addition to the cruelty-free happy childhood superintended by parents devoted to each other – of another source of psychological warping which I might have been able to endlessly mine for creative purposes. The instances where strange men took an unhealthy interest in the youthful me were few and far between – two, in fact, and about seven years in apart. The first time was when, at the age of 11 and school-capped, blazered and short-trousered, I was taking the short, two-stop train ride from Ewell West to my home station of Worcester Park.

Trains then had closed compartments – two upholstered bench seats facing each other, with a door on either side. Once inside, there was no leaving the compartment, other than when the train stopped in a station. One afternoon, I got in an empty compartment, only to be followed into it by a thirtysomething man in a business suit. I was mildly surprised when, with the compartment otherwise empty, he sat next to me, and said that he, too, had been at my school (a line, I suspect, which was not true but his chosen way of breaking the conversational ice with small boys). I was even more surprised by what came next. He asked if he could put a personal question to me, and I agreed, assuming this would be something along the lines of 'Do you like football?' or 'Have you got a stamp collection?' But the question was not about sport or philately. It was: 'Do you have hairs between your legs?', and it was the sly manner in which he made the inquiry, rather than its subject matter, that made me uncomfortable. But, being 11 and unversed in the ways of child-tamperers, I was not so uncomfortable that I declined to answer. I heard myself (disturbing encounters often seeming like out-of-body experiences) reply along the lines that there were the beginnings, but not yet a full crop. Fortunately, before he could follow this up with an even more startling inquiry, the train pulled into Worcester Park station and I got out, leaving my questioner to continue his journey, which, fortunately, he did.

It was only as I walked home, going over this strange encounter in my mind, that it occurred to me that he may not have been telling the truth when he said he was an old boy of Glyn Grammar School, soliciting small boys for descriptions of their genitals probably not, I decided, a usual part of the freemasonry of going to the same school. I was untraumatised (no actual liberties having been taken), and, the odd times I've recalled the incident, wondered what else I could have done. Pulled the communication cord (the equivalent then of the emergency alarm buttons now on trains)? Jumped to my feet, called him a disgraceful pervert, and told him I would report him to the authorities? Or, more likely, shyly refused to answer his question? I would not have either dared pull the cord ('Penalty for misuse £50' said the sign), or had the brass neck to report him. And refusing to answer grown-ups when they asked you a question (even one about the state of your undercarriage) wasn't something that life up to then had prepared me.

It would have been about seven years later, when I was between school and university, that the other occasion occurred. My father, determined that I should earn some money in the ten months between getting a place at Cambridge and actually going there, had obtained a white-collar dogsbody job for me with Mobil Oil Company, for whom he worked. I was to be a bag-carrier and figure-adder-upper for management scientists while they ran the rule over some part of Mobil's UK operations. The first assignment was at oil terminals in Ellesmere Port, Merseyside, and, since it would inconvenience the management expert if he was in a swanky Liverpool hotel while I was in a B&B in New Brighton (as would have befitted my lowly status), I was booked into the Adelphi, the city's finest, and once the overnight stay of choice for first-class passengers taking White Star liners across the Atlantic. I went ahead as the advance guard, and so, aged 18, I arrived in Liverpool on a wet January night and, amid the mahogany, polished brass and chandeliers of the Adelphi's lobby, checked in.

I had an evening meal, and afterwards went to the cocktail lounge, intending to order a Coca-Cola and take this and my book to a corner. But before I could do so, I was spoken to by a chubby, middle-aged man sitting on a stool at the bar. He insisted on buying me a drink. He was 'in helicopters', he told me, and staying at the hotel for one night after concluding a 'big deal'. He seemed pleasant enough, and so I stayed chatting to him. It was only when he asked for my room number that the dreadful penny dropped. And it was only when I heard myself tell him the number that I started to become alarmed. Trying not to show the panic I felt, I said I needed the Gents, which luckily was in the same direction as the lifts. Once out of the lounge, I bolted for the lift, got to my floor, ran down the corridor, locked the door behind me, and, fearing that this may not be enough to deter the helicopter man should his sexual rotors be now going full pelt, manhandled a heavy wooden chest of drawers across the room to the doorway and sat there in the dark, lest a slither of light under the door betray my presence within. The precautions were not necessary. No knock ever came. But it cost me a good hotel breakfast, the embarrassment of seeing him again sending me out into the chilly Liverpool morning long before that meal was served. I had a bacon roll in a café instead. Men with designs on me never reappeared; women with designs on me never cropped up in the first place.

The only time that I was cast in the role of deviant was in 1983 when, working for *The Observer*, I was covering the Open Golf Championship at Royal Birkdale as a sidekick to Peter Dobereiner, the paper's golf writer. We found ourselves, such was the skill of the paper's staff at booking accommodation, not in en suite hotel rooms with a view apiece of the sea but sharing a chalet in Pontin's holiday camp at Ainsdale Beach. Late one night we fell to discussing my golf grip. My right hand, Dobbers insisted, was too strong and needed to be more on top of the shaft. Producing a club, he pulled a mattress onto the floor and insisted I swung repeatedly at it as hard as possible.

This being Pontin's, where the continence of the guests was evidently not to be relied upon, the mattress was plastic-covered. The noise it produced when struck forcibly by an eight-iron was both satisfactory and loud; and each swipe was accompanied by Dobbers' shouts of encouragement. It never occurred to us how this might sound to a neighbour through the thin chalet walls. But, while the sound of strenuous fornicating or the hurling of crockery during some holiday argument might have passed unremarked upon in Pontin's, the noise we were making did not: a loud 'Thwack!', followed by a male voice shouting with some passion, 'Harder! Go on, harder!' Some sort of representations by the neighbours must have been made, for the following morning a Pontin's official appeared at our door saying that there had been 'reports of goings-on here last night'. As he spoke, he peered over our shoulders to the room beyond, fearing, I suppose, that he would see manacles, or even, perhaps, a tethered goat. He said he'd been told of loud and unusual noises coming from our chalet, at which the penny dropped, and we explained what we'd been doing. It seemed to us, a pair of golf enthusiasts, a perfectly normal way to spend a late evening. But not to him. What upset him was not the nocturnal noises but our abuse of a Pontin's mattress. He left, warning us that our deposit may have to be forfeited, as indeed it was, one of the stranger entries I've ever had to make on an expenses form.

ELEVEN

art and artlessness in the suburbs

Trips to the cinema might have been the major mass out-of-home entertainment in the 1950s, but they didn't loom very large in the Randall scheme of things. Dad never went, and Mum only took us to the pictures once or twice. We grew up ignorant of Hollywood, and, if someone had asked us what the Rank Organisation did, we'd have said they produced flour. So no sitting in the red plush seats of the one-and-nines, lapping up a double-bill as we sucked on a Kia-Ora orange juice through a noisy straw. No stampede down the aisles for the ice cream queue at the interval. No main feature, no corny ads for the Taj Mahal restaurant 'just a short walk from this cinema', and not even the Pathé News cockerel crowing before footage of the latest royal tour was shown.

Years later, I wondered why, when almost everyone else was at the Odeon or Essoldo once a week, we were not. Part of it was that Dad, working longish hours and sometimes bringing work home, was pretty protective of his relaxation time, preferring to spend it pottering at home rather than gadding about. He was also a bit of a fidget. I doubt his attention span would have been up to a couple of hours sitting in a darkened cinema, unable to have a magazine on his lap as he always did when watching television. But the main reason for the failure of cinema (or theatre and concert hall, for that matter) to lure him in was that Dad was born into, grew up with and had always revelled in a tradition of making your own entertainment. Its origins lay in the remarkable Christmas Day show put on at his parents' terraced house in Wandsworth every year. Even in the sing-songs-round-the-piano days when it was performed (about 1909–39), the annual family Variety bill was thought extraordinary. December evenings in his childhood were spent making scenery (painted on the reverse of old wallpaper and stuck on a draught screen), being rigorously rehearsed by Grandad Randall and Uncle Douglas, and helping his father produce via a gelatine stencil a souvenir programme with running order, mock advertisements about family foibles and a lucky number for the post-show raffle.

Come mid-evening on the great day, the audience would be seated expectantly on hard wooden forms in the bay, while the cast of five, wearing lurid make-up which rendered them faintly luminous for days afterwards, waited in the 'wings' (in reality, the hallway). On the stroke of eight, the curtain (an old sheet) parted to reveal the orchestra: Dad, then still in short trousers, as percussionist, armed with small drum, triangle and cymbal, plus his cousin Hettie on the old upright piano. As the cheers died down, they burst into the overture of 'Blaze Away'. There followed fully forty minutes of sketches, topical songs, monologues, conjuring tricks and a one-act (so-called, as the programme explained, because only one of the cast actually could) drama. The humour, based chiefly on recent misadventures of various members of the audience, translates imperfectly now, but, at the time, guaranteed much stamping of feet and demands for more at the end of the show. This was just as well, since Grandfather's programme always stipulated that 'performers will not vacate the stage until an encore has been requested'.

These celebrations were made possible, as so much family togetherness was in those days, by all branches living within a few streets of each other. The exception – Dad's Uncle Joe and family at Peckham Rye – used the 37 bus, which in those days ran until midnight on Christmas Day. Having brothers and sisters, grandparents, cousins, uncles and aunts all living nearby enabled everyday borrowings and returnings, impromptu outings, emergency child-mindings, gatherings on the Common for cricket and picnics, and many casual callings on each other. After the war, it all changed. Grandad Randall and Uncle Douglas were dead, and the family redistributed about south London, Surrey and Kent. Mick and I knew large family Christmases, but these involved car journeys and were after-lunch affairs. No more would the Randall men, as they had done for decades, repair to the front room after Christmas dinner, select easy chairs and sleep off their meal while keeping an occasional eye on their individual small candles on the mantelpiece. Each candle would have 6*d* beside it, and the owner of the last candle alight would collect all the money.

Anyone daring to come into the room would be shouted at in case they caused a draught and blew somebody's candle out. The family Christmas show had guttered and died, too, and eventually – as Dad's generation aged, and his sister Doris and her husband directed their social gaze towards friends and neighbours rather than family – gatherings of the whole clan simply ceased to happen at all. Only funerals would ever bring them all together. When, eventually, the last of them filled the coffin in question, there were no more of that generation to bind the wider family together. The descendants of this once inseparable tribe exchanged Christmas cards, but had little real contact, save for me and my cousins James and Andrew, with whom I share a sense of humour as well as a bloodline.

(We were inducted into the family tradition of performing at an early age when Dad coached Mick and me for our first, and, as it turned out, only appearance before an audience together. It was at Bracklesham Bay Holiday Camp in West Sussex, where, in addition to a weekly campers' concert for holidaying show-offs, there was, each Thursday afternoon, a children's version. We were 5 and, dressed in matching shorts, jerseys and sandals, took to the stage. We were shepherded to the microphone stand and invited to give our party piece. It was a short, comic rhyme that Dad had taught us. Our tiny, amplified voices sang out the words, and we finished, gave our bows, then – silence. Dad's idea of comedy, it turned out, was a little too racy even for a holiday camp, and the female compere felt compelled to apologise. We left the stage to a mere smattering of weak applause, and the shuffling of our own small footsteps, amid the low-level murmurs of audience discontent familiar to anyone who has ever performed and been found wanting.)

ART

Mum and Dad were no art lovers, not even part of the 'I don't know much about painting but I know what I like' brigade. I never knew them to visit a gallery, express an opinion or buy so much as a framed print of a much-visited holiday spot. They were, in a literal sense, artless, and the proof was on their walls – or, rather, not on their walls, since these were virtually bare of pictures, save for two gifts: the print of a schooner cutting through the waves in full rig, and a watercolour of cricket on a village green. The first was a mystery, since there was nothing nautical about our family or its forebears. The village green tableau was explained by Dad's love of cricket, and a reminder to him not only of many an afternoon bowling off-breaks, but also of his favourite novel (indeed, the only one he ever read): *How Our Village Beat the Australians* by Hugh de Selincourt. Little did Dad know (or would have cared) that de Selincourt is now more famous for his sex life, chalking up affairs with, among other obliging women, Margaret Sanger, the American birth control campaigner and part-time mistress of H.G. Wells, and Francoise Lafitte Cyon, the woman who reportedly cured pioneer sexologist Havelock Ellis of impotence by allowing him to watch her urinate – a spectator sport which de Selincourt sensibly omitted from his books.

While Mum and Dad's art-blindness fully fitted the metropolitan view of the suburbs as a sort of tribal reservation for philistines, they were not typical. Quite a few of our friends' homes seemed to go in for pictures in a big way, and, whatever you might make of their choices, there was no doubt they brought some life and interest to their walls that ours so conspicuously lacked. One picture was puzzlingly popular, hanging over the mantlepieces of three different friends or relatives. It was that cliché of 1950s and 1960s homes, *The Chinese Girl*, a 1951 portrait of a young oriental woman with a greenish face and an incomplete background which looked as if the artist went to answer the door mid-picture and never returned to the canvas. The door-answerer was Vladimir Tretchikoff, a Russian émigré who had lived in Shanghai and Singapore before moving to South Africa. Here he found 17-year-old Monika Pon working in her uncle's launderette, and paid her £6 to sit for him and be immortalised as the Chinese girl. When it was finished, she objected to the green face. 'It makes me look ill,' she told

Tretchikoff. Five years later, Woolworths were selling framed repros for £2 a time. Huge numbers bought it, untroubled – perhaps even reassured – by the ferocious condemnation of art critics. William Feaver, for instance, called it 'the most unpleasant work of art to be published in the twentieth century'. In 2013, the original was sold by Bonhams for £982,050. As for the repro, the picture duly faded from suburban fashion. In the late 2010s, copies could still be had for a pound or two at boot fairs and charity shops.

The only other picture allowed on our walls was a framed piece of marquetry in the hall. It had been done by our Auntie Doris, who had what was called 'an artistic side', then not a euphemism for unwelcome behaviour. This village scene pieced together in different coloured woods was an example of something common in homes then, less so now: homemade stuff. In our own: handkerchiefs and antimacassars embroidered by Grandma Randall's sister Hettie, a shed of lapped wood made by Dad, and a fair amount of Mum's handiwork: cross-stitch pictures of flowers, a shag-pile rug, tea cosies, pullovers, boiled egg covers, soft toys and knitted gloves. When we were very young we even had swimming trunks she had knitted – fetching to her eyes, perhaps, and certainly unusual, but less than practical once the bather had ventured into the sea. Weighed down by salt water, they felt as if they were liable at any moment to collapse around the ankles.

They didn't, thanks to sturdy elastic threaded around the waist.

Little of this home handiwork was prompted by the need to save money. Women of that generation and income bracket nearly all stopped work when they got married, and, aside from keeping home and raising children, they knitted, sewed, embroidered, wove, dress-made, cross-stitched, darned and poker-worked. Partly a hangover from the make-do-and-mend war years, it was also the exercising of a skill, the pleasure in seeing the family wear or use something they had made, tangible evidence of the value of these non-wage-earners to the household, or, at the very least, proof to their husbands that they had not spent the post-housework day curled up on the sofa with a page-turner of a romantic novel and a box of peppermint creams.

Mum was a great knitter. I wore her sweaters until my early 20s, and the moment I stopped doing so can be precisely dated – not because I kept an obsessive record of what I wore, but for rather more shameful reasons. At Cambridge, I was involved with the Union Society, and a television crew came to make a documentary about the then-president of the Union, Arianna Stassinopoulos (later Huffington), a striking, statuesque young woman of Greek origin who buzzed about the town in a red sports car, and, even then, was a relentless networker of the famous, whose ranks she would soon join. I was a small, lowly rock in her orbit, and so, at one point in the resultant film, I was asked to shuffle in from stage left, clutching some papers or other for her attention. I watched the broadcast in a crowded college bar, and saw this figure resembling me enter the picture wearing one of Mum's pullovers: blue, with thin horizontal white stripes. I heard a snigger several rows behind, and can feel even now, nearly fifty years after the event, the warm prickle of embarrassment that here, in the purlieu of sophisticates, was this man wearing a jumper so obviously knitted by his mum. It is entirely possible that the snigger was prompted by something else entirely. But in my mind it was the sound of the suave spotting a suburban interloper. I never wore her pullovers again.

MUSIC

Dad's favourite music was the songs of the 1920s and 1930s (his teens and 20s), especially when crooned by the Cliff Adams Singers in a radio programme of close harmonies called *Sing Something Simple*. This, coming out of the Roberts radio from its home on the shelf in the kitchen, is the sound to me of early winter Sunday evenings before the tea things were cleared away, and everyone else migrated to the back room for television leaving me to do my homework on the kitchen table. Until Mick and I got a Dansette record player and started to buy 45rpm discs, these decades-old hits, plus whatever was sung on TV variety shows, were pretty much the only music I knew. Music lessons at grammar school consisted of trying to teach us to coax a tune from a recorder. In my hands the recorder never became a musical instrument but remained a tube of wood with holes in it. What was almost never done in our lessons with the small and fussy Charles Cleall, the school music master, was any attempt to introduce us to what might be heard in a concert hall, be it symphonies, sonatas, fugues, choral ensembles, jazz, big bands or concertos. I left school at 18 totally ignorant of the world's historical music, apart from the sugary croonings of Cliff Adams and his Singers, Dad's limited repertoire of Al Jolson and George Formby hits strummed on his ukulele, and the odd hymn sung in assembly.

What put this right was a girl. Her name was Mary Ann Slade, whom we have already met briefly, a mathematician of whom I was inordinately fond throughout most of my time at Cambridge. Early on, when we were getting to know each other, she mentioned that her mother sang in the London Philharmonic Choir, and wondered if I'd like to come and hear them perform Fauré's *Requiem*. I'd barely heard of requiems, never mind Fauré, but such was my keenness to spend time with Mary Ann that I said yes. An hour or so of boredom would be a fair price to pay for the chance of a bit of après concert canoodling. My first evening in a concert hall passed less onerously than I'd feared, although I was a little disconcerted to find that, unlike the cinema, you couldn't smoke. Still, things were going nicely with Mary Ann, and I agreed to go to another concert, inspired less by the music than the thought of more progress on the romantic front. As the first item on the menu began, I steeled myself for a further session of pretending to enjoy the music. But, within a few minutes, I found myself swept along by it. 'What is this?' I whispered to Mary Ann. She pointed to the programme: Tchaikovsky's *Violin Concerto in D major*. And hearing its stirring but plaintive sounds was one of those revelations when a hitherto closed door opens and sets you on a path to discover endless delights. From that evening on I wallowed in classical music, or, at least, the syrupy sweet romantic part of it. No one had ever gone to a concert with baser motives; no one had ever left so rewarded by finding unknown treasure.

Mary Ann, who tired of me shortly after I graduated, provided by far the most shocking experience of my college days. One afternoon, we had parted in the centre of Cambridge and she went off towards her college, Girton, which was a couple of miles away. I went back to my room and was working when, early that evening, two men came to see me. They were detectives. Mary Ann had been attacked on a path beside the busy Huntingdon Road. A man had come up behind her, thrown the poncho she was wearing over her head, pulled her to the ground, and began punching her and scrabbling at her clothes, ripping them. Had a cyclist not come along and disturbed him, worse would no doubt have happened. These details I learned later, the police at first merely telling me she'd been attacked and then asking me questions clearly designed to rule me out of – or into – their inquiries. They were stern and persistent, but, once satisfied, their mood changed, and they ran me in their car up to Girton to see Mary Ann. She was bruised, had a tooth or two damaged, but seemed surprisingly calm. That didn't last. She soon began talking excitedly about everything and nothing, mostly the latter, and it struck even an insensitive clod like me that it would be best if she was not left alone that night. When her chatter finally subsided, she lay back on the bed and fell asleep. I sat in a chair, occasionally dozing but mainly not. In the small hours, Mary Ann suddenly sat up and stared dead ahead. I spoke. No response. It was as if she was in a trance. A few minutes of this and she subsided slowly back and slept. This happened twice more that night.

By morning her mother had driven up from their distant home and, in due course, I told her of Mary Ann's catatonic state in the night. She was grateful that I'd been there, but furious that the college had provided little by way of care for a young woman who'd been viciously attacked.

In the course of giving some official a piece of her considerable and understandably agitated mind, she said: 'Why, her boyfriend had to stay with her last night.' The reaction was immediate and horrified. 'Her boyfriend stayed the night in college!' Girton, I hope, has since made progress on the student welfare front. Mary Ann, who was made of formidable stuff, recovered and went on to build a happy life for herself, her husband and their three sons. I discovered this when, forty-five years on, for the purposes of this book, I tracked her down and checked that she was happy for me to tell the above story.

BOOKS

School was school. I neither liked it, nor disliked it. I was, however, by the time I went at the age of 5, prepared for it. During a childhood illness some months before, which kept me in bed for a couple of weeks, Mum had taught me the rudiments of reading. So I was able to deal with our first school's reading material: the *Janet and John* books, which, for all their almost fanatically Home Counties atmosphere, were actually Anglicised versions of the original American books, called *Alice and Jerry*. They were heavily illustrated and consisted of simple sentences describing the domestic doings of an 'ideal' family: 'See, Janet helps Mummy in the kitchen.' 'Look. Daddy and

John make a toy boat.' Janet and John were neat, tidy and polite at all times, a pair of insufferable goody-goodies. How one wished for them to drop a plate when washing up, throw a tantrum round the shops, or scoff all the chocolate biscuits and be sick on the carpet. What subsequently earned them scorn, however, was not this, but their gender stereotyping: she the little apprentice housewife, he doing all the interesting stuff with Daddy involving hammering, chiselling and other such manly activities. Hence the rewritten and re-illustrated updates that have appeared. Janet now gets a fair crack of the screwdriver and grease gun, while John does a bit of sewing and pastry-making. The baleful influence of sexual typecasting was, of course, lost on us – indeed, pretty much lost on everyone. As far as gender roles were then concerned, the *Janet and John* books were pure documentary: in the suburbs, home was female, work was male, and little boys and girls were expected to follow these set tramlines. And horrified though progressive minds might be at these books now, they sold in their millions and helped entire generations to read. Many a gender studies professor's literacy must have begun with Janet and John's imbecilities.

The first books I really relished were Enid Blyton's *The Faraway Tree* stories, harmless little fantasies about three children who discover in a vast soaring tree a variety of characters, some entertaining, some frightening. There was

Moonface, the Saucepan Man, Mr Whatsisname, the Angry Pixie and Dame Slap (the latter now bowdlerised in modern versions into Dame Snap, who no longer slaps children but merely chides them, thus becoming a bit of a nag rather than a character to fear). I knew them first when Mum read them to me, and it was wanting to savour them on my own that spurred me on to read. This must have been the experience of huge numbers of children, and you would think this would make Blyton a hero to teachers and educators, her portrait hung in many a library to honour this author of 762 books who set so many children on the road to a lifetime's reading.

But there were – are – two problems with Blyton's output. First, there was her use of golliwogs – little black dolls obviously based on what my grandparents would have called 'pickaninnies' – as the naughty villains in the *Noddy* books. It's fair to say that Blyton may have seen black children as some sort of aberration. In one story of hers, Sambo is shunned by his owner and the other toys because of his 'ugly black face', and only welcomed by them after a shower of rain washes his face 'clean' and makes him as pink-faced as the others. You don't have to be black yourself to recoil. Most of Blyton's output included no such characters, but racism was not the only reason critics attacked her work and succeeded in getting it banned from schools and libraries. They saw it as simplistic, using a restricted vocabulary, and tantamount, according to literary critic Margery Fisher, to giving children 'slow poison'. Yet her stories, with idioms updated and a certain amount of revision to remove what now reads as snobbish, outmoded or risible (characters such as Dick and Fanny now renamed Frannie and Rick), continue to sell in vast quantities.

What no longer fly off the shelves are the kinds of books I moved on to next: stories set in boarding schools. I read a few of Anthony Buckeridge's *Jennings* yarns, set in Linbury Court prep school, but they lacked a certain fizz compared with my favourite: the *Greyfriars* stories. These had, among the cast, several grotesques who would not have disgraced Dickens: Mr Quelch, schoolmaster, classicist and cane-wielder much given to long, solitary country walks (where he went, and what he did on them, left tantalisingly unanswered); William Gosling, surly boy-hating school porter; and Mrs Mimble, the tuck shop proprietor. But chief among these was Billy Bunter, the greedy, obese, lying, cheating, thieving anti-hero, based partly on author Charles Hamilton's brother Alex, a dismally unsuccessful freelance journalist who, in the absence of any publication fees turning up, was a perpetual scrounger. Hamilton, who wrote the stories under the name Frank Richards, was a good cut above the writers of similar yarns, having a sort of sub-Wodehouse turn of phrase and not being averse to indulging in a tinge or two of irony.

Why did I, and millions of other boys, read stories about boarding schools? In his essay 'Boys' Weeklies', George Orwell wrote that stories set in public schools were popular because they let young readers into an unobtainable world they fantasised about being part of. According to Orwell, the boys absorbed in a *Greyfriars* book, or girls lapping up another *Mallory Towers* adventure, were like those who now drool over magazines devoted to exotic sports cars or multi-million-pound country houses – experiencing vicariously what they will never be able to do in reality. He wrote: 'It is quite clear that there are tens and scores of thousands of people to whom every detail of life at a "posh" public school is wildly thrilling and romantic. They happen to be outside that mystic world of quadrangles and house-colours, but they can yearn after it, day-dream about it, live mentally in it for hours at a stretch.'

I'm not exactly sure that the Old Etonian is right. A certain amount of wistful envy may have been at work, but it was not the sort that Orwell fancied. I was never bothered that the stories were set in a school not remotely like my own, nor that the children in Enid Blyton's *Famous Five* and *Secret Seven* books never seemed to holiday in boarding houses, but in some relative's large seaside house overlooking a sandy cove used by smugglers. Relevance was the last thing I wanted from a book, and I was no more troubled by the stories failing to reflect life as I knew it than the fan of science fiction is put off by alien happenings on the planet Tharg bearing little similarity to their own existence in Market Harborough or Bolton. The story was what mattered, and the vital ingredient, it seems to me now, was the absence of parents. Home life, families (rich or wayward uncles apart) and the small change of domesticity were entirely absent, thus freeing the characters to get up to the kinds of tricks that those of us living in more mundane settings lacked the freedom to imitate. This, I think, was where the envy came in. We weren't (or, at least, I wasn't) coveting the alleged privilege of being sent away to school to win house colours, be preyed upon by bullies or pederasts, have midnight feasts, or wear a boater. Nor were we wishing our mum and dad had the wealth needed to pay the fees. We just thought of all the fun and mischief you could have when you inhabit a world free of parents. The only thing I yearned for, to borrow Orwell's word, was to have the chance to track sinister foreign criminals, discover treasure in coastal caves and have parentless slap-up teas, with lashings of lemonade and cake.

And that is why, I suppose, stories set in domestic surroundings, such as Richmal Crompton's *Just William* books, had little appeal. Nor did anything with a military or nautical flavour. Boys I knew devoured the *Biggles* books, but war was not something I ever wanted to read about, however thrillingly (or sanitised) it was portrayed. Besides, war stories were likely to be set overseas. There would be unfamiliar landscapes, odd-sounding place names, and buildings that were all too obviously foreign – lots of steeply sloping roofs, tiles of unusual hues, shutters over windows, etc. This was always off-putting to me. I much preferred stories to have an English setting, with cosily familiar hills, woods, villages and townscapes. It is, I suppose, another manifestation of a suburban lack of any sense of adventure, a wariness of anything untried, and an unease about the foreign. These must be the reasons why the first adult books I read were Agatha Christie's murder mysteries, always preferring the very English Miss Marple to the fussy little Belgian, Hercule Poirot. Here, amid thatched cottages, vicarages, and manor houses, were easily digested characters (retired colonels, family black sheep, spinsters, pretty young women with expectations, their uncertain suitors, etc.) populating plots that took a bit of following, but were not too grown-up on the psychological front. Old Agatha's books zipped along at a snappy pace, her characters never going in for much in the way of page-clogging navel-gazing. And, once I'd had my fill of reading about the likes of Mrs Inglethorpe, Colonel Protheroe, Miss Pinkerton, Rex Fortesque et al being bumped off, it was an easy glide down the fiction slipway to P.G. Wodehouse, and so to A level set books for exams, and Orwell and his like for pleasure.

Library books apart, there were only three books in the house before I started buying and stockpiling them: *The AA Book of the Road*, *Readers' Digest Book of Gardening* ('why not try shrubs to create winter interest?') and a novel by Warwick Deeping, published in an era when male authors were pictured on the inside of the back jacket, looking vaguely thoughtful and holding a pipe. Deeping was an exception to this visual cliché. With his round, rimless spectacles and sunken-cheeked face, he had instead the look of an underfed Gestapo officer. He thrived in the age of circulating libraries (even Boots the Chemists lent books in the 1920s and 1930s) when writers could earn a decent living turning out short stories and barely disguised copies of their previous books. Deeping was a qualified doctor who served in the Army Medical Corps at Gallipoli and on the Western Front during the First World War. He wrote seventy-two books, but had to wait until his thirty-third before he had a bestseller, which is about thirty-two more chances than a modern novelist would get. Quite what his novel was doing on Mum and Dad's shelves I never knew. He was not their sort of writer; Dad only ever read magazines and car manuals, and Mum preferred romances from the library. Her favourites were historical novels with titles like *The House at Cupid's Cross*, *Evergreen Gallant* and *Believe The Heart* by the likes of Jean Plaidy, Phillipia Carr and Victoria Holt. Mum probably never knew, nor would have cared had she done so, that these women were one and the same person: Eleanor Hibbert, the daughter of a book-loving dock labourer who became a one-woman novel factory. She had several more literary aliases, and, by means of being able to knock out 5,000 words by lunchtime, produced 200 books. She died on a cruise ship and was buried at sea. Mum's other preferred author was Georgette Heyer, a name which sounds like a nom-de-plume but was not. Born in Wimbledon, she married a mining engineer and was a prolific producer of historical novels and thrillers, fuelled by the sixty to eighty cigarettes she smoked each day. She was pathologically private and never gave an interview, unlike many of today's authors who seem to do little else.

Mum and I were regular borrowers at the library, walking the quarter of a mile or so to our branch at least once a week. It was an unusual foundation, even for the outer suburbs, set in a couple of acres known as Shadbolt Park, named for a retired director of railway construction in India whose garden and grounds they had formerly been. Ernest Shadbolt was a collector of rare plants and trees, with good contacts at Kew, and the result was that the way to the library was through a miniature arboretum, each specimen neatly and clearly labelled. The library was in Shadbolt's former house, a neo-Georgian doll's house of a thing, kept for him by his niece, Miss Brimble. It was bought for a library the year after his death in 1936, and it was up its steps and through the entrance porch that Mum and I would go with last week's borrowings – some read, others tried and found wanting – and emerge a while later with fresh supplies. Thus, courtesy of Epsom and Ewell Borough Council and the days when enabling the pleasures of reading was thought as much a municipal duty as the provision of drains, did I begin a lifetime immersed in books.

Dad's regular reading, car manuals apart, was *Reader's Digest*, to which he subscribed, meaning we did not have to wait until visiting the doctor or dentist to sample its offerings. Easy to mock (which I shall do in a moment), it did introduce me at an early age to the world of grown-up reading. Here were articles on current affairs ('Richard M. Nixon – A Hero For Our Times' or 'Charles de Gaulle, France's Man of Destiny'), technology ('Computers Are The Future!'), family life ('Getting Through To Your Teenager') and suburban etiquette ('Casual Dress Codes: Have They Gone Too Far?'). Health seemed an especial preoccupation, and each month's issue contained a whole four weeks' worth of worry-fodder: 'Tinnitus: Terror In Your Ear', 'Are You A Diabetic?' or 'Herpes, Scourge of the Sexual Revolution', an article which, if memory serves, reported with barely disguised glee on the downside to that particular event. It also had a feature entitled 'Humour Is The Best Medicine', in which the editors collected quotations and anecdotes which, by even the loosest of yardsticks, were not remotely funny. There were also, for the non-doctors among us, articles that explained the workings of various bits of the human body. They were headlined something like 'I Am John's Spleen', or 'I Am Elizabeth's Adrenal Gland', but never, annoyingly for teenage boys like me, 'I Am Samantha's Reproductive Parts'. Thus was my knowledge of physiology confined to what could be discussed among mixed company in the grill room of a Maryland country club. But, for all its faults, *Reader's Digest* did suggest to me once a month that the world contained lots of interesting things I'd never previously heard of. And, since we're giving it at least some credit, it was the first mainstream publication to report, in the mid 1950s, on the link between smoking and lung cancer. This was partly, I suppose, due to its near-fanatical health mission, but also because in those days it carried no advertising and so it could, unlike most other papers and magazines, relay the US Surgeon-General's misgiving about fags without the risk of losing lucrative ads from the cigarette makers.

TWELVE

suburban shopping

The retailers of Worcester Park were concentrated on Central Road, half a mile of shops that lined the hill as it climbed from the station to the beginnings of North Cheam. As you left the station and turned south, there was a small parade of single-storey shops, not much bigger than kiosks in some cases: a hairdressers, florists, coal merchants and estate agents. The coal merchants was our favourite, not because we had any interest in domestic fuel, but because it had in its window a model railway and, when a penny was put in a slot, a train would begin to run round. Close by was a fabric and fashions establishment opened by Mrs Boddington (of 'High Trees' fame, described in Chapter Five). It was called Polly Esther, because, at the time it opened, that material was all the go, and the shop's proprietor hoped that passing housewives would be lured in by a name which suggested that here, a door or so down from where you ordered your anthracite, latest fashions from the pages of *Vogue* could be had at affordable prices. Sadly for her, however, polyester soon came to be thought of as the textile equivalent of Formica.

Thus began the main Central Road shops which, occasional forays on the 213 bus to Kingston apart, were our entire retail universe when I was a child. There were no fast food outlets, or charity shops (neither of these things existed), and only a few premises – Caters, Victor Value, David Grieg's and Woolworths – were part of chains.

None of these have survived, all either merged, taken over or faded into receivership. Branches of Woolworths, when I first knew them in the 1950s, had red and gold facias, mahogany counters with glass dividers, and wooden-floored aisles whose straightness offered such direct and easy egress for the shoplifter. Woolies sold useful items – screws, light bulbs, curtain fittings, tableware – of decent quality, if uninspiring design. The rot set in after they plunged into self-service, did away with counters and the helpful assistants behind them, and plonked the name Winfield on everything they sold. They thus offered consumers the unique experience of buying drain cleaner, saucepans, writing paper, ant killer, shirts, ties, bras and perfume all bearing the same brand name. The consumer was not impressed.

David Grieg the grocers was a shop whose methods were, in the Fifties and Sixties, essentially unchanged from Edwardian times. Butter, for instance, was not sold in packets, but cut from a long block, and patted into sellable shape by a woman wielding two wooden bats with grooves on their inner faces. Everything was behind glass cases and counters, two of which ran the length of the shop either side of a black and white tiled aisle. You asked for something then handed over your money, which was put into a sealable metal canister connected to wires and a tug given. The canister containing your money and a note of the price was whisked along to a cash kiosk at the far end, the correct change put into the canister, and a tug at that end sent it back to the assistant who served you. It sounds a long-winded process, mainly because it was. Griegs was far from unique. Freeman's, the haberdashers and soft furnishings shop across the road, used a similar system of canisters, wires and pulleys.

We never called such branches of a chain 'stores', an Americanism put into common currency by marketing folk trying to suggest their businesses were bigger and better-staffed than they were. They were just 'the shops', and most were run by owners who knew their suburban customers and went to what we would now think of as excessive lengths to keep their business. Dad, for example, because of his job as a sales manager for Mobil Oil Company, was required to send large numbers of Christmas cards. And so, every early November, a small, moustachioed man called Mr Fowler of Fowler's the stationers would call at our home with books of samples from which Dad would select that year's card. These would duly be printed with 'Season's Greetings' and Dad's name. Mr Fowler's profit margin, I imagine, was small, but it kept the better class of customers happy and ensured that Mum, when in need of a pencil or eraser, would patronise Fowler's, where she would be greeted as if she were part of the local gentry.

Mr Fowler combined fussiness with a slightly exaggerated deference towards customers, but then this was true of most of the shopkeepers, their eagerness to please a large part of what kept them in business. And, in the days before the chains and discount houses took over the high street, it worked. This approach was certainly true of Mr Frisby, whose shoe shop Mum used for our boyhood needs, although her and my father's taste for high-quality footwear (one of their few extravagances) was catered for elsewhere. The shop had very little footwear on display inside the shop, but the walls were stacked with boxes and boxes from floor to ceiling. The ritual when we entered never changed, Mum directing Mr Frisby to offer us only the most sensible and hard-wearing items in unpatterned black leather. We would emerge a while later in footwear so unfashionable we could have been child actors in a costume drama set fifty years earlier. The one concession to the passage of half a century was that we were allowed, around the age of 11, to have snake belts. These were narrow, elastic belts, horizontally striped in two garish and conflicting colours (crimson and an unpleasant shade of yellow, for instance) that had two metal interlocking S-shape clasps embossed to make them resemble a snake. These belts were not needed to keep the trousers up, but an adornment, our first accessory, i.e. an article of clothing that had no purpose other than to be shown off. For a time, these were the acme of schoolboy cool, the getting of a snake belt being a sign that you were approaching that prized milestone of childhood – leaving it and becoming a teenager.

The defining feature of most shops was their counter. The hardware shop, for instance, had a particularly formidable wooden barrier between you and most of its stock. Behind it stood a pair of men in dark blue storeman's coats who heard your request for a certain length and type of nail, screw or household component, and found it in their ceiling-high array of drawers. Screws and nails, etc., were sold loose, in small paper bags; very little in the shop was pre-packaged. This was true of sweet shops, too. Chocolates came in boxes and bars in their wrappers, but most loose sweets such as humbugs, mint imperials, various kinds of caramels, etc., were not in factory-made bags. Why would they be? Shops had assistants to explain, serve, weigh and bag, and no one but the supermarket companies had yet worked out that the savings through self-service and fewer shop assistants would more than outweigh any loss from increased pilfering.

The barrier between goods and customer that counters and assistants erected cannot be exaggerated. You couldn't handle a possible purchase unless you asked an assistant to produce it for you, which sometimes took a lengthy rummage by them in the stockroom. Only shoppers of a certain self-confidence would do this and then reject the item, but even at the age of 9, I was that shopper, especially when in our local toy shop, Elliott & James. When we had birthday or Christmas money to spend, my brother Mick and I would enter their shop with all the swagger of gunslingers entering the frontier saloon. Walking the gauntlet of bikes, trikes and other large toys, we would make straight for the objects of our desire: Corgi and Dinky cars, die-cast models to a scale of 1:43 kept under a glass-topped counter. On the wall behind were shelf after shelf of more models in their boxes. Mick's eyes would quickly alight on a car in the display and he'd buy it. I would ask for car after car to be put on the counter so I could inspect, and then invariably reject, it. I'd ask to see the catalogues, identify possible purchases, a ladder would be produced, models retrieved from the upper shelves by Ernie, the long-suffering shop assistant, and these would be examined. It was not unknown, after all this rigmarole, for me to exit the shop empty-handed, saying: 'I'll think about it.'

Some of the expeditions to Central Road filled us with foreboding, among them visits to the dentist, whose surgery was reached by a steep flight of stairs that, for all the reluctance with which I mounted them, might as well have been the steps up to a gallows. Mr Horan was our dentist, an Irishman who seemed nice enough until he started to practise his trade on you. An extraction meant being knocked out with gas, a process that began with the pungent smell of the rubber mask as it was held over your face. The idea was that you would then subside into gaseous oblivion. In fact, the terror you had been feeling for days, the effect of the anaesthetic, and what was left of your functioning brain being dimly aware of the violence being done to you, induced nightmarish dreams. Mr Horan's female but muscular assistant often had to hold me down. Fillings were a less nasty palaver, but far from a picnic. However, once the medieval implements had been laid down, and you had rinsed your bloody mouth out with the pink water, there came a bizarre conclusion. Mr Horan would reward you, if you'd not kicked up too much of a fuss, with a tube of Smarties or packet of boiled sweets – a serious shot of sugar which, added to what you routinely consumed, would ensure your next visit would not be all that long in coming. This wasn't their intention. It was just that Mr Horan and sidekick were so pleased to see me off the premises each time.

The other dreaded outing was to have your hair done. Boys in our era did not go to hairdressers, let alone hair stylists, but to barbers. Ours was in a side-street off Central Road on the first floor of a building called Jonah House. It had three barber's chairs facing mirrors, some worn leather benches for waiting customers, and by these, on a low table, the usual small heap of much-thumbed old magazines. A couple of glass cabinets containing various hair oils and packets of razor blades completed the interior that was, in its fittings, essentially unchanged since the 1930s – as was the approach to hair styling of its proprietor and sole haircutter. He was a fierce-looking man in a short white coat who sported a Hitler-like toothbrush moustache and a short back and sides that would not have looked out of place on a recent Waffen SS recruit. No cheery banter here, indeed no talk at all, just the *clip-clip* of the scissors interspersed with periodic loud sniffs from the miserable man wielding them. To grown-up customers he may have traded football talk, or tips for the 3.30 at Sandown Park, but I doubt it. He probably didn't even proffer the famed 'anything for the weekend, sir?' enquiry. (This, a euphemism even small boys could decode, was a way of asking customers if they wanted any condoms in the pre-pill days when it was thought that married couples only had sex at the weekend.) Hitler the hairdresser seemed an unlikely purveyor of these prophylactics. After all, if he was having such a lowering time, why should anyone else have any fun?

Being made to go to the shops with Mum was sometimes used as a sort of low-level punishment for some minor misdemeanour, the domestic equivalent of lines rather than a detention. You were required to do nothing more disagreeable than pull Mum's shopping trolley (a severe enough sentence should a schoolfriend be met), but the worst part of it was the waiting. Whole fragments of my childhood were spent outside the wool shop while Mum went inside to discuss her knitting needs, and hardly less time was spent kicking my heels while Mum disappeared into Barclay's to get some money out. To a child, and no doubt to the less financially confident customers, banks in those days were forbidding places – dark interiors when seen from the street, windows of frosted glass, and, inside, all mahogany counters and brass grilles, behind which were the staff – as distant, it seemed to us, as the money they guarded as if it were their own. Unlike today, customers were not seduced, lured, offered 'products', leaflets or inducements to transfer their accounts, or indeed their affections, but simply unsmilingly tolerated. The general impression given by banks was that they were doing you a favour by allowing you to lodge your money with them, which seems more honest than today, when they purport to be your friend or therapist.

But Worcester Park was only the local parade. Shopping proper, shopping with a capital S, meant a trip on the 213 bus to Kingston, where there were two special attractions: Bentalls department store, and the Green Shield Stamps shop. Green Shield Stamps were the customer rewards scheme of the day, similar to today's loyalty cards but minus the sneaky data collection. At shops and garages, you got a stamp for every 6*d* (two and half new pence) you spent. These were stuck in stapled booklets and eventually redeemed for goods shown in the Green Shield Stamp catalogue, which told you how many books of stamps you needed for each item. A set of coasters might only be a book and half, kitchen scales might need four books, whereas a Ford Cortina car cost 1,350 books and a Mirror sailing dingy eighty-four.

Within a few years of the trading stamp idea coming to Britain in 1958, the first thing many people would ask when going into a shop was: 'Do you give Green Shield Stamps?' Parents with children in school, Scout groups, Girl Guides, etc. began pooling their books so they could get sports equipment or a couple of new tents for the annual camp, and the people at Green Shield were able to tell you how many books you needed for almost anything. The Hertfordshire congregation of a Catholic church even managed to collect enough stamps to get their priest a new set of Mass vestments in each of the liturgical colours. Mum confined herself to small items for house and garden, although we were once allowed to choose what to get and plumped for a fishing rod. So it was off, with more than the usual sense of anticipation, to the Green Shield Stamp shop. This was more like the left-luggage department at a railway station than a store: a light, airy hall where you queued, told staff behind a long counter what you wanted, presented your stamp books for inspection, got a ticket, and sat and waited for your number to be displayed on a large illuminated board, which was the signal to go to the counter and collect your item.

It felt like something for nothing, but the shops and garages paid to be Green Shield Stamp outlets, and no doubt passed that cost on to customers. What did it for Green Shield was a combination of the ever-rising inflation of the 1970s (it hit a peak in 1975 with an average for the year of 24.2 per cent) and supermarkets deciding to attract custom by diverting the fees they were paying for the stamps to give discounts. Green Shield Stamps stopped being issued in 1991, and the business turned itself into Argos, whose shops are strongly reminiscent of the old stamp redemptions hall we used to go to in Kingston.

Just a few hundred yards away from Green Shield was the entrance to Bentalls. Here was a department store in the old style: an enormous emporium selling everything we could think of, and much that we couldn't, with facilities for account customers (no vulgar handling of cash for them), deliveries via the store's bright-green vans, and soberly dressed staff to serve you – the men in sombre suits, the women in black skirts and cream blouses. Deference here was a way of life. Inside Bentalls, Mum became 'Madam', and even I became 'the young gentleman'. The forelock-tugging didn't end there. In December 1970, I got a job at Bentalls in my first university vacation, and saw from the inside the workings of an old family-run store. When Mr Rowan Bentall, grandson of the founder, did his rounds, the older female staff all but dropped a curtsey as he passed. Slightly shocking to the modern mind, there was actually a charm about what lay behind this. Bentalls may not have paid top-dollar in wages, but they had a care for their people which, to the hard-nosed types who run retail businesses today, would be even more shocking. There were Bentalls clubs for sports and chess, a Bentalls choir, a good pension scheme, and a staff restaurant that dispensed decent two-course lunches for 6*d* (not even three pence in today's money).

For shoppers, Bentalls had two sources of refreshment: a self-service café on the ground floor and, on one of the upper floors, a silver-service restaurant. Here, those who fancied themselves descendants of the old carriage class would repair for luncheon, or high tea. They were mainly women, or ladies as we would have been taught to call them then, the word 'woman' or 'women' being regarded in the suburbs as vaguely demeaning. Washerwomen were women, chars were women, shop assistants were women, but wives who did not work were ladies, and they were the mainstay of the Bentalls restaurant. Handbags would be hung from the tables on decorative hooks, gloves removed (but not hats), and feet aching from all the shops they had walked through would be rested and revived. Until at least the 1970s, it was a scene that was positively Edwardian. Clothes and prices apart, it could have been Derry and Toms, or Liberty's, circa 1909.

In the suburbs – indeed, for everyone bar the very well off – eating and drinking out was far less common in the 1950s and '60s than it later became. There were, for instance, no coffee shops. People got up, had breakfast, went straight to work and had to wait until a tea break or, if they worked in an office, go unbeveraged until the tea lady came round mid-morning with her urn and trolley. No Costa, Starbucks, Pret; no people bustling about, plastic-lidded coffee cup in hand. Nor, for that matter, going everywhere from April to November with a bottle of overpriced water ostentatiously clutched. People just took less liquid, I suppose. Apart from pubs, al fresco refreshment was available only at transport cafes (always pronounced 'caff'), or tea-rooms (the plural invariably used, even though the establishment nearly always only had one room). In my childhood, every shopping centre and parade in the outer suburbs had its tea-rooms, and Worcester Park's was entirely typical.

Called Marigold's, it affected, with its half-timbered façade, doll's house window frames and Olde Englishe lettering above the door, to look as if it were a Tudor relic amid the utilitarian stone and brick of the 1930s parade of shops. It wasn't, of course, but like almost all tea-rooms of the period it felt it had to look like a suburban cousin of Ann Hathaway's cottage. There would be fake beams down walls and across ceilings, a plate rack full of chintzy knick-knacks, framed Marjorie Allingham-style pictures of rose-covered country cottages and be-smocked yokels, red-checked cloths on the tables, and elderly waitresses in cream blouses and black skirts with little white pinnies. These things, and especially the checked tablecloths, were signs to Mum and Dad that here were available an acceptable cup (and definitely not a mug) of tea and a slice of reasonably fresh cake. Freshness, especially in places that looked as if they were struggling, needed constant vigilance. Women like Mum were adept, or gave the impression of being so, at identifying staleness in the cakes on offer by a simple glance at them under their glass-domed covers. 'That Victoria sponge wasn't made today, I know,' would come the verdict from half a dozen paces away, and so we had to have the dark and grown-up-tasting fruit cake rather than the yellowish and delicious sponge and its jammy filling. Buttercream was reserved only for butterfly cakes, and had yet to begin its career of ruining the traditional icing-topped cupcake. Eccles cakes we avoided.

A sure sign to Mum and Dad of the better class of tea-rooms was that the menu came in a leatherette cover, and, prior to being handed over, was preceded by the ridiculous question: 'Would you like to see the menu?' The alternative, presumably, being to sit there and hazard guesses at what might be available. These superior rooms would also do light lunches (Welsh rarebit and the like), and maybe even run, for special occasions, to a plate of fancies (small iced cakes that were half sponge, half fondant, and always sounded more alluring in the ordering than they tasted in the eating). The tea always came in a pot, and was only of one kind: English breakfast. You had to go to a four-star hotel if you wanted to order Earl Grey, and there was no sign (indeed most of us had never heard of them) of green, mint or chamomile teas. The only coffee was what we would later call an Americano with milk, although classier rooms would offer a cafetière. What we now call lattes or cappuccinos were known as 'frothy coffees'. They were available only in coffee bars, which were a London phenomenon we'd distantly heard about, far more Soho than suburbia. And the one thing you could rely on about Worcester Park – and still can – is that it had very little in common with Soho. It was, and is, twinned instead, spiritually and physically, with thousands of similar urban outliers all over Britain. Unchic and, in fancy circles, unloved and even a little despised, they are Anywhere, UK; and also Everywhere, UK. Millions of us live in them. Hurrah for the suburbs!

a suburban inheritance

You may or may not inherit money or heirlooms, but the one thing we all have passed down to us are genes and, if parent or parents remain alive through our childhood, some sort of tradition and culture, likely, in good measure, to be very similar to what they knew as children. That will be your inheritance. For anyone who wants to place what I have written in some sort of ancestral context, I come from a long line of people of the lower middle-ranking sort (millers, weavers, shoemakers, etc.), who were born, got married, had children, died, and did very little else worth mentioning. They may have been cruel, kind, saintly or complete shits, but we'll never know. They never did anything good, or bad, enough to trouble history's scorers. Where they can be found in the official record, they live on only as names, dates, addresses and occupations. It's a kind of immortality, I suppose, but to spare my four grandparents such a mere bare bones remembrance, here is what we know of the characters of those who, with Mum and Dad, made my brother and me the suburban sorts we are:

Mum's father was born Percy Stuart Plaice in King's Lynn, Norfolk, in 1886 to a rather mysterious pair who married only a year or so before. His mother, Charlotte Collins, brought three daughters – all born out of wedlock – to the household; of his father we know only his name, James, and occupation, labourer. He died after only a few years, and Percy was apprenticed to a compositor and moved to London in his late teens. He married in 1911. Even in his 70s, Percy was a strikingly handsome man, and he was not one to waste these good looks. Such was his womanising that his wife said of him and women: 'One was not enough, and ten not too many.' He certainly carried on with women at work and at one time his wife bustled along to his office to confront him and his current lady friend, a Gladys Ost, spinster daughter of a sweet shop owner. Five years after his wife died, he married this Gladys and moved to a bungalow in Rainham, Kent. We were very fond of him, but frequent and prolonged non-speakers between him and Mum meant that after our 7th birthdays we saw him only rarely. All later attempts to find out from Mum the reason for these lengthy stand-offs were met with her standard response to anything to do with her family: 'What do you want to know for?' In the end we put them down to her resentment at Percy's womanising and the way he led his first wife, her mother, such an unmerry dance. He later moved to Sudbury, Suffolk, where he died at the age of 82.

We were very fond of this skilled calligrapher, who would, on the rare occasions we saw him, act as a sort of co-conspirator with us against whatever it was that Mum was currently saying 'no' to, whether it was another slice of cake or a later bedtime. And he had a good imagination. Once, when with us, he said he had a stomach ache. 'What's it like?' we asked. 'Well,' he said, 'stomach aches are blue, you see.' And, taking a pen, Grandad drew a cartoon of it. We wanted to go to his funeral, but were told it was 'not necessary'. It was a shame, but what really rankles is the thought that when his childless second wife died nineteen years later, all Grandad's drawings and exquisite lettering would have been binned by the house-clearers. All we have by way of keepsake is his service medal for the First World War, commemorating the eighteen months he spent in the Royal Flying Corps. No doubt, in the course of cutting a swathe through the obliging women of SW19, he may have occasionally given the impression that he spent 1917–18 in a Sopwith

Camel dicing with the Red Baron, rather than, as he actually was, shuffling documents in the RFC's clerical section.

Mum's reluctance to speak of the past meant that it was only after her death that we discovered Percy had a brother – Mum's Uncle Jack – who married in 1909 and took his bride off to Australia. He served in the Australian Imperial Army in Flanders, was wounded, and left shell-shocked. He had two daughters, both of whom died childless. In 1939, he came to Britain and stayed for several weeks with Percy. Mum, who would have been about 21 at the time and still living at home, never mentioned the existence of 'Uncle Jack', whose signature we later found in her autograph book. Odd of her, but entirely in keeping with her reticence about anything to do with her family. We learned she also had an Uncle John on her mother's side who ran a café in Reigate – again, no mention. The one exception to this radio silence was her mother's sister Ada, who married and emigrated to Canada. Mum wrote to her regularly. Her daughter and husband visited Britain when middle-aged, and stayed with us for a day or two. Her husband talked constantly of the marvels of Canada and the drawbacks of Britain. Dad did not encourage him to stay a minute longer than was absolutely necessary.

Percy's wife, Mum's mum, was Florence Emily Edgson from Hillingdon, Middlesex. I have her engagement photograph from 1911. She sits erect and clear-eyed, smiling straight at the camera, a beautiful young woman in a dark, flounced skirt and elaborate blouse who could have been the daughter of a banker, rather than, as she was, that of a bricklayer's labourer. Fewer than thirty years later, there is another photograph, taken at Mum and Dad's wedding in 1940. She had become a thin-lipped, pinch-faced, bespectacled woman who, at 50, looked at least twenty years older. For her, as for so many women outside the wealthy classes, middle age seemed to hardly exist. You were either youngish or oldish, with no intermediate stage in between. In fewer than thirty years, young Florence Emily had turned into old Flo. This may have been medical, the misery caused by Percy's philanderings, or the heartache of losing two baby boys in infancy. (A third survived, Mum's beloved brother Dennis, but he died of peritonitis at 16.) The loss of these boys may have been the reason why Grandma Plaice doted on Mick and me when we arrived. But that wasn't to last long, for she died of leukaemia before our 2nd birthday. When she became ill and was told by a doctor she would have to remain in hospital, she told him: 'I don't care what you do to me. Give me shit, or give me sugar, but get me back to my kids (meaning us).' When she was admitted for the final time, Mum used to wheel Mick and me in our double pram to the hospital grounds so she could wave to us from her ward window. I'd like to think we waved back. Of all our recent ancestors, she – a very warm-hearted woman, according to Dad – is the one I would most like to have known.

Dad's father, Alfred William Randall, we never knew at all. He was born in 1881 and died at 59 in 1940 of a heart attack prompted by a landmine explosion near his Wandsworth home. He was a supervisor with the Imperial Cable & Wireless Company, and a talented cricketer (bowling for the Civil Service, Surrey Club and Ground, and Malden Wanderers). A teetotaller, he looks serious and unblinking out of formal photographs, as if he didn't have a humorous fibre in his being. But the camera misleads. He was the master of ceremonies at the famed old-times Randall family Christmases (see Chapter Eleven), and a considerable practical joker. An example: one year, by way of a change, the hard core of the Randall Christmas revellers decamped to Brighton where his wife's cousins, Uncle Alf and Aunt Lou, had opened a guest house called 'Kisara' in Bloomsbury Place. Despite its exotic name, this establishment prided itself on its wholesome family atmosphere. Imagine, therefore, the dismay of paying guests as they entered the residents' lounge one evening to find that Grandad Randall and several other male relations of their landlady appeared to have turned it into a gambling den They were seated tensely in shirt-sleeves and eye-shades, desperately engaged in a card game at a table on which were piled considerable quantities of silver coins and pound notes. It was all that Uncle Alf could do to persuade his shocked clientele that the degenerate tableau was just his relatives' little joke.

Alfred William was devoted (overly so, some said) to the constant happiness of his wife, our Grandma Randall. She was born Jessie Edith Dorr, the youngest child of Conrad Dorr, a German who emigrated to Britain as a teenager. He was an instrument maker with premises in Long Acre, near to Leicester Square, and, when I began to root around in genealogy, I thought there was a chance my brother or I might unearth a Dorr violin or cello. It took no more than a look at the 1871 census returns to realise that the instruments he made were not musical but surgical. A bit of a let-down, a Dorr truss not having quite the same ring to it, although hernia sufferers might disagree. In 1864, Conrad married a young Suffolk woman, who died in childbirth ten years later. Within a year, he wed Louisa Ann Green, the daughter of a Hertfordshire baker, and started a large family in Battersea. His youngest child of seven, Jessie Edith, our grandma, was only 6 months old when he died at 47. Less than two months later, all the children were taken to St Luke's, Battersea, to be baptised, indicating that Conrad was either a militant atheist, Roman Catholic or Jewish. A more practical explanation is offered by what happened next – all the children, except one, were distributed to various institutions for orphans, a state then defined as a child missing merely one parent. Grandma Randall's sister, Hettie, for instance, went to the Lambeth Orphanage, where she learnt the needlework she was still employing in her 80s. None of these places were run by the Church, but baptism may well have been a qualification, if only to prove the children did not come from an entirely godless family. Jessie Edith remained at home with her mother, who went out to work in a shop. The demeanour of the youngest, favoured 'baby' of the family never left her, according to our mum. When we knew her, Grandma Randall would already have been widowed some fifteen years or so. Her home was in Berber Road, Wandsworth, a street of terraced Victorian villas. She died in 1964, and a decade or two later City and media types began to move into the area. Chi-chi restaurants, delicatessens and fireplace shops opened, and property prices rose spectacularly. In October 2014, the house next door to hers, no doubt much improved in the meantime, was sold for £1.1 million, a startling increase on the £3,300 Dad and his sister accepted for Grandma's fifty years before.

Dad was active and buoyant until the day he died, aged 79. He went to sleep on a windy evening in January 1990, had a massive heart attack, fell out of bed and, according to the doctor, was probably dead before he hit the floor. His funeral was an object lesson in how not to do it. At the time I was regularly giving after-dinner speeches. I wanted to speak about

Dad at the service, but was afraid my brother Mick would think I was trying to turn the funeral into the David Randall Show. I decided to stay in the pews and let a locum clergyman say a few words. Despite a briefing from us, he got Dad's name wrong, and added a few bits of twaddle of his own manufacture. My wife had to restrain me from rising to my feet, telling this bumbler to sit down, and delivering the tribute I'd wanted to. There was no chance of this being repeated when Mum's turn came. Mick and I wrote and delivered a double-act salute to both of them.

Mum lived on in widowhood for a further sixteen years, gradually losing her sight and moving into a care home. You had to forcibly remind yourself, when impatient with her slow, Zimmer-framed progress about the place, that this was a woman who had once run for Middlesex and who, in mothers' races at school sports days and the like, would line up against the be-shorted, plimsoled competitive types and, in just street shoes and an A-line dress, romp home the winner. She enjoyed the care home, and we visited at least weekly, but she grew ever more feeble until about the only thing she could do for herself was breathe. At the age of 87, she finally stopped doing even that.

You may also enjoy ...

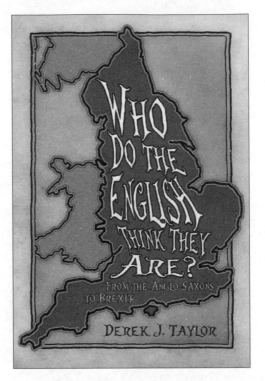

978 0 7509 8915 2

A nation's character is moulded by its history, and Derek J. Taylor travels the length and breadth of the country to find answers.

Faced with uncharted waters post-Brexit, what is it in their national character that will help guide the English people?

A 1960s Childhood

From Thunderbirds to Beatlemania

PAUL FEENEY

978 0 7524 5012 4

Do you remember Beatlemania? Radio Caroline? Mods and Rockers? The very first miniskirts? Then the chances are you were born in or around 1960. Take a nostalgic look at what it was like to grow up during the sixties and recapture all aspects of life back then.

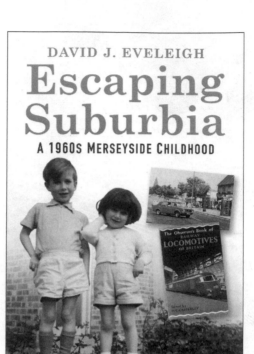

DAVID J. EVELEIGH

Escaping Suburbia

A 1960S MERSEYSIDE CHILDHOOD

978 0 7509 9239 8

With a vivid eye for detail and boundless childhood curiosity for everything from steam trains to 'My Old Man's a Dustman', *Escaping Suburbia* documents the uneasy relationship between worlds old and new and offers a different perspective on the 'swinging' sixties.